It Was Beginning to Seem as Though We Might Be on the Outskirts of Civilization. . . .

Forty miles below Fisher's cabin we came to another cabin. The old man who lived there, Clark, fixed us moose steak and filled us with stories. He had come north during the gold rush of '89. He told of men striking it rich and men who died trying.

"Come over the hump from the Yukon," he told us, and I asked if he had come by way of Rat River. He shook his gray tousled head, smiled wickedly, drawled, "Yep. She a bastard. If you're going that way it's a 1,400-foot climb in forty miles. Bald-faced mountains. Wind howls. Deerflies as big as your thumb, and mosquitoes draw blood a pint at a time."

We had photographs of the Rat River, given us by the flyboys from Fort Smith; the country appeared brown and desolate, and the river a squiggly white line of uninterrupted rapids. The Rat was going to be our toughest challenge. . . .

"*NEW YORK TO NOME* is a rip-roaring seat-of-the-pants adventure . . . extroverted and direct. . . . Taylor recalls his adventures with the relish and equanimity of one truly inspired by the challenges of surviving in the wild."

— *Sea History*

NEW YORK TO NOME

THE NORTHWEST PASSAGE BY CANOE

RICK STEBER
FROM THE RECOLLECTIONS OF SHELL TAYLOR

POCKET BOOKS

New York   London   Toronto   Sydney   Tokyo

POCKET BOOKS, a division of Simon & Schuster Inc.
1230 Avenue of the Americas, New York, NY 10020

Copyright © 1987 by Rick Steber

Published by arrangement with North River Press
Library of Congress Catalog Card Number: 87-24035

ISBN: 0-671-67871-X

First Pocket Books trade paperback printing August 1989

10 9 8 7 6 5 4 3 2 1

POCKET and colophon are trademarks
of Simon & Schuster Inc.

Printed in the U.S.A.

NEW
YORK
TO
NOME

PART ONE

CHAPTER 1

1936. We were mired in the depression. Living with FDR and the New Deal. Prohibition had ended. Women wore hats. George Burns, Gracie Allen, Bing Crosby, Jack Benny and Will Rogers were on the radio. It was the era of big bands. Clark Gable, W.C. Fields, Claudette Colbert and Belle Davis were in the movies. The parking meter had just been invented. Passenger cars had hood ornaments, running boards and cost under a thousand bucks. Ninety percent of rural America was without electricity and indoor plumbing. We had ice boxes, very few refrigerators; radio but no television. The world had survived the war to end all wars. Germany was retooling under Adolph Hitler. Americans were not as naive as we had been.

More than anything this was the golden age of exploration. We were pushing back the last frontiers, searching corners of our planet never seen by civilized man: flying over the Poles, venturing into the heart of Africa, the back country of Australia, the Amazon jungles. The newspapers and newsreels were full of it.

1936. I was walking up Broadway in New York City with Jeff Pope, a good-looking, gangly kid who worked at the desk across from mine in the circulation department of Macfadden Publications. We were clerks.

It was February, a cold, gray dismal day. The stench of the city was trapped at the surface by a temperature inversion. I was doubting myself—why had I ever come to New York? I was fed up with cabs and buses and drivers yelling to get out the rear door; going up and down in elevators when all I wanted was to get outside and away from the hubbub, which, of course, I could never escape.

The snow was filthy with winter soot and garbage. God, how

3

I despised it and wished I were back in California, the state of my birth. I longed to smell the wind fresh off the Pacific rustling the tops of ancient redwood trees, taste the tang of salt and hear the bullfrogs croaking along the banks of the Russian River. Crickets, too.

I had come to New York several years before, seeking fame and fortune, but found myself stuck in a dead-end job. I could look around and see how lucky I was to have even that. There were two million unemployed aimlessly wandering the city, pausing to warm themselves from burn barrels along the streets. Perhaps I should have felt content but I was young and ambitious, definitely going to the top, although my ascent was not happening as fast as I had planned.

Jeff and I caught lunch at one of those joints where you paid a dime for a glass of beer and they allowed you a free sandwich. On the way to the office I felt the beer and ham on rye sloshing in my stomach. From Broadway, where we were walking, it was impossible to see the Hudson River but for some unapparent reason—to this day I do not know how the idea germinated or how long it lay there before taking root—I imagined myself in a canoe on the Hudson River. I blurted, "Wouldn't it be fantastic to quit our jobs, get in a canoe and follow that bloody river wherever it goes!"

Jeff looked at me with that shocked expression he was so famous for, as if I had said, "Ol' buddy, why don't you and I take a quick trip to the moon." Jesus, all I had said was it would be great to jump in a canoe and go, leave New York and all the crap behind.

Despite Jeff's dour attitude I could not help but carry the idea further. I said, "What an adventure!" In my mind I was paddling, with an easy current and the sun on my face. It was marvelous, just as it had been in California. As a teenager, I had run a trap line with a canoe on the Russian River.

In the elevator going to our floor I thought about my experiences, and at my desk, instead of settling down to the work at hand, I flipped open an atlas to see where the Hudson River headed. Lake Champlain. I envisioned a large body of blue water, shoreline fringed with sandy beaches and woods crowding close. Was that what it looked like?

And then, inadvertently, I discovered Lake Champlain was connected by a waterway to the St. Lawrence River. The St. Lawrence led to the Great Lakes. I traced across splotches of blue and followed squiggly blue lines. My finger swung north to Lake Winnipeg and hopped from lake to lake across Saskatchewan to the Slave River, Great Slave Lake. . . . I whispered each revelation across to Jeff. He was not working, either intent on watching me, or simply interested in my discoveries. The Mackenzie River led from Great Slave Lake and we could run that all the way to the Arctic Ocean. But wait! I backed up. If you took the Rat River you could make a short portage to the Yukon drainage, and it was a downhill shot to the Pacific Ocean.

I leaned back, momentarily stunned by the magnitude of the discovery, reeling at the implications. I lit a cigarette, blew smoke, and informed Jeff, "This is a big deal—a Northwest Passage. Henry Hudson, Sir Francis Drake, Alexander Mackenzie searched for it, searched in vain. Maybe this isn't the route to open trade with the Orient, but it is a waterway connecting the Atlantic to the Pacific. The continent, without a doubt, can be traversed by water." I thought to myself what made this revelation possible were modern-day maps. Only in the past decade had aerial photographs been available to map makers.

Joe Wiegers, our boss, came through the door at the far end of the long room. He would pass our desks on the way to his office. I closed the atlas and whispered to Jeff, "If you want to check this out, if you're interested, meet me at the Fifth Avenue Library. Seven."

I was a spring wound too tight. From the cursory examination, it appeared quite possible to traverse the continent from coast to coast with only a minimum of portages. What an unbelievable trip that would be!

I gave it about a fifty-fifty chance Jeff would meet me. If he did, it would be because he was intrigued with my zeal. This idea had me rolling. I was totally enthralled. What possibilities!

When I got to the library I had to ask directions to the map room. I was up to my elbows in maps when I glanced over to see Jeff seated at the table across from me.

"Didn't think I'd make it, did you?" he said. I let it slide.

Jeff, at age twenty-two, was two years younger than I. He was a solid six-footer, had me by several inches, but the major difference between us was not measured in years or inches. I was easily entertained and my funny bone ran deep. Jeff, to put it bluntly, lacked a sense of humor.

Jeff had started to work at Macfadden Publications six months prior to me. One day Wiegers called Jeff into his office and I thought, "Oh boy, Wiegers is on to him," because I did the majority of the work. To give an example, Jeff had a habit of lighting a cigarette and leaving it in his ashtray. He would sit with a straight back, looking like he was working, and that damn cigarette would burn all the way to ash. He would be sound asleep. And when he was asleep he was dead to the world. That is the truth. What did Wiegers do but give Jeff an anniversary raise, two bucks a week.

"What for?" I asked Jeff. "I tell you what, if you give me your raise I'll do all your work. You just have to do enough to make it look good."

Crazy, but he went for it. He said, "Beautiful." The deal was struck.

That was a pretty good example of the dissimilarities between Jeff and me. I was a turned-on guy. I liked to work. I hustled and I rattled the cage. Jeff was laid back. He was easygoing. He was a tortoise. To him money was unimportant. Me, I wanted the money. I wanted a better apartment, better clothes, a new wrist watch, the chance to take my girl friend to dinner. I wanted the two bucks. Hell, I wanted four. I wanted a thousand.

Before they blinked the lights to let us know the library was closing in ten minutes, Jeff and I had set a course up the Hudson River to the Pacific Ocean. We had taken books from another section of the library and used them to lay out the route taken by the fur brigades. Routes of men like Alexander Mackenzie who had gone from Montreal as far as the Arctic Ocean. We would retrace the trail he had blazed and do one better. We would reach the Pacific Ocean, something no other man had ever done. I asked myself how many men ever have a vision of historical importance. If there was any time in my life when I could chase a dream, this was it. I was footloose with nothing to tie me down.

Just before closing the map book, I noticed that up the coast from the mouth of the Yukon River was the settlement of Nome. It struck me what an excellent ring "New York to Nome" had. On the way downstairs I told Jeff. We stood on the sidewalk, Fifth Avenue noisy behind us, talking and probing the possibilities of undertaking such an expedition. I was actually starting to see myself as a serious candidate to verify the Northwest Passage.

"Why don't we grab a drink and discuss this a little further?" I suggested, and Jeff was agreeable.

We went in the first bar we came to. Jeff told the bartender we would take beer but I changed it to brandy, telling Jeff brandy helped the thought process. He shrugged. It was his manner to shrug. I hated it. At the office I would ask him where the Montana ledgers were and he would shrug. Monday morning I would ask what he had done over the weekend, a civil gesture, and he would shrug.

It had occurred to me Jeff might not make the ideal expedition partner. Of course, his faults were mostly superficial, petty things. Big deal. So he shrugged. I sipped the brandy and felt its slow flush. For a moment my thinking became muddy and tenuous. I reprimanded myself—how could I even consider such an undertaking? New York to Nome I estimated to be 7,000 miles, with 150 miles of portages. That was 150 miles carrying heavy packs and a canoe. One man would never stand a chance. It would take a team. But Jeff?

We had several brandies, and the alcohol obscured my normally clear judgment. I sat there, skin feeling taut. What an astonishing thing, the human body. In simplest terms I was merely muscles, bones, glands and a brain. Would I have a chance to cross the continent? Hell yes! I had the drive to finish anything I set out to do.

I took another sip of brandy. My throat felt constricted and my tear ducts overwhelmed. My perceptions were changing. My world was changing. The bar was smooth under my fingertips. The blue cloud of stale cigarette and cigar smoke overhead became a storm of bitter disappointments, business deals that would fall through and dreams never realized. Was this mere fantasy—a trip by canoe across the continent? I wanted realism, challenge, conquest. I told myself, "If you don't do it, you're a candy ass." That did it. I ordered another round.

I drank brandy, told Jeff, "I feel like a snake shedding his skin." He had no idea what I was talking about, and I could not bring myself to come right out and say I was definitely thinking about committing myself to attempt the expedition. I was not ready. I was sorting through friends and acquaintances and measuring them against Jeff to see if I could discover a better companion. But each person had to be crossed off. Some were married and a few had families. They could never get away. Others were set in a career or had a steady girl friend. Jeff was looking better all the time. I tried to categorize those things about him that annoyed me. Funny, at that moment nothing about him seemed insurmountable, except for his lack of a sense of humor. That bothered me. The other things could be worked out or maybe overlooked.

The brandy gave me courage. I looked at Jeff. His hazel eyes flickered like a mink's at knife point. I think he sensed my announcement even before I made it. The loon was out there somewhere in the fog on a lonely, unnamed lake, its voice a long, uncoiling wail. Somewhere between laughter and madness. I had never seen a loon but now I knew I would.

I hoisted my brandy snifter, proposed a toast. "I hereby swear to go the distance, reach Nome, or die trying." I admit I was a bit melodramatic, but I was consumed by the challenge to succeed where no man had. And the brandy was partially to blame.

To my utter astonishment, Jeff, who had been playing devil's advocate by saying things like, "Anyone kicking a good job in the rear at this point in time is crazy," suddenly reversed. He clinked his glass with mine and repeated the vow, to go the distance, reach Nome, or die trying.

Pop-goes-the-weasel. I had a partner. I was not sure if I was glad or not, but I admired the hell out of Jeff's commitment. Our names would be forever linked in history books. Shell Taylor and Jeff Pope.

The enormity of the expedition bobbed to the surface and I felt a quick shiver run the length of my spine. I told Jeff, my voice carrying the gravity of the situation, "We have to start planning. There are letters to write. We have to research the best ways to survive in the bush. We need maps, money, a canoe, grub, gear...."

We had another brandy and debated the best publisher to sign with. And there undoubtedly would be a movie in it.

CHAPTER 2

I slept with my window open, a carry-over, I suppose, from my younger days in the country. In New York I was awakened by the garbage truck grinding along the street and the clatter and clank of cans as they were dumped and returned to the sidewalk. Sometimes I stood in front of the window, stretching, watching them, and the sun would be coming up over the city. The light was soiled, not like I remembered it in California.

Jeff and I spent the weeks following our commitment to the expedition focusing on research: writing letters and requesting maps and information from various branches of the Canadian government. At work my fingers would do what had to be done, but my mind would wander to the myriad details to be attended to if we were to get away by early spring.

For the most part Jeff and I were getting along famously. He was every bit as awakened as I to our great calling. I might suggest something and it was done. I never had to mention it twice. That fact impressed me. He was a hard worker when he wanted to be.

That was not to say everything was rosy.

Jeff and I had clashes. For instance. I was a Lucky smoker and Jeff was strictly a Chesterfield man, nothing but Chesterfields. His habit was to run out of cigarettes, complain he was out and wait for me to offer him a Lucky. Then he would turn up his nose and say something like, "Me, smoke a Lucky? Not on your life."

One day I told him, "I'll bet you a five spot if you smoked a Lucky you would like it." He made a terrible face as if the very thought sickened him, retorted, "You're on, because I'll never sink low enough to smoke a Lucky. I'd rather do without."

I didn't say any more. After work, on the way to the apartment, I bought a pack of Chesterfields and spent a good half hour carefully extracting tobacco from a Chesterfield into one pile and a Lucky into another. Then I inserted the Lucky paper inside the Chesterfield paper and filled it with the Lucky tobacco.

Right on schedule in the middle of the afternoon Jeff ran out of cigarettes. I produced my pack of Chesterfields, explained the store had been out of Luckies, and offered him one. I made sure he took the one I wanted. He popped it between his lips without the least suspicion, lit it, took a long puff, let it out slowly and commented something about the unmistakable quality of fine tobacco, saying I ought to permanently switch to his brand.

"Do you really like it?" I pressed.

"Of course," he replied and then, catching his first inkling that I was tricking him, looked at the cigarette to make sure it was a Chesterfield. From outward appearances, it was, and I let him think so. He nodded.

"You're sure?"

"Yeh, I'm sure."

"Well, then pay me the five bucks," I said, telling him to tear off the top paper and he would find a Lucky. He refused to take my word. I am sure my little subterfuge embarrassed him. But it served him right, as if my brand were not good enough for him.

There was another incident that happened during the same period which caused a minor rift between us. It involved a girl in the office. Her name was Sidney. She was a very good-looking gal, and it just so happened we were dating. We never brought our romance to the office. I thought office romances were tacky and so did Sidney. We had fun away from work, but at the office we were all business. No patty-cake or pitty-pat. Oh, maybe I would give her a discreet little wink when she passed my desk, but no different than I did with any of the other gals who worked for Macfadden.

The amusing offshoot to our deception was that Jeff was arduously attracted to Sidney. In fact, he had asked her out several times but, of course, she always evaded going on a date with him.

Jeff and I usually had lunch together and we would talk about how things were going. On Sidney's birthday, I told Jeff I had personal things to attend to and would not be going to lunch with him.

"I think I'll skip lunch, too. I'm not very hungry," he told me and brashly suggested, "Maybe I'll just tag along with you."

"Suit yourself," I bristled. "But I don't want you to ever come back on me and give me a bad time."

We hiked to Macy's, and I bought Sidney an initialed brooch.

It was beautiful and impressed Jeff, I'm sure. That evening I took Sidney to dinner and gave it to her.

She showed up for work the next day wearing the brooch. Jeff spotted it right off the bat. There was no mistaking it. I was watching him. Red slowly crept up his neck and flooded his face. He was gnashing his teeth. He came over to me and snapped, "You bought it for Sidney. She's your girl friend, isn't she?" Jeff had made some comments in the past about Sidney, about how he would like to get her in the sack. Right then I thought he was being way too sensitive. All I said was, "Our agreement was I let you go on the condition you never come back on me or give me a bad time." There was nothing he could say. It was just as well.

There was no reason whatsoever to think Jeff and I should mesh perfectly. We were two very different personalities from diverse backgrounds. I was a fifth-generation Californian, reared on a farm on the Russian River, a country boy at heart; although I had read every book I could get my hands on and learned at an early age that intelligent conversation is one of the greatest pleasures in life. Jeff was a city boy from Minneapolis—not that that was anything against him, but there are things a city boy just can't know the same way a country boy can: fishing, hunting, trapping, using certain tools. My father was a master of everything. He taught me mechanics, and I did all the mechanic work on the farm. I had a block and tackle in an oak tree, and could pull an engine, tear it apart, and put it back together. I could hitch a team of horses and plow a field. Jeff didn't know the difference between a hame and a halter.

In mid-March there was a sportsman show at Grand Central Palace. I mentioned to Jeff we should plan on attending; it would be a perfect opportunity to price a canoe and gear.

We went on Saturday, the final day of the show, and spent the afternoon wandering through the maze of booths sponsored by the major outdoor equipment manufacturers. We visited with the representatives of both Peterborough and Chestnut canoes, discussing the advantages and disadvantages of each particular model. I was in the middle of pitching the Chestnut agent, thinking his company might be willing to give us a canoe for the exposure they would get, when I was interrupted by the public address announcer, "Your attention please. We have a special treat for your enjoyment this evening. Famous radio commentator, Floyd Gibbons, will be hosting his national show from center stage of Grand Central Palace. Be sure to stay for that."

11

The Chestnut agent was hemming and hawing, and I could tell he did not have the authority to give away a canoe. And then it hit me. I was off and running. We needed money, sponsors, media exposure. What a perfect opportunity! We would get on Gibbons' show.

I grabbed Jeff's arm and pulled him in the direction of the stage. When we got there, Floyd Gibbons with his eye patch was an easily recognizable figure.

I marched up, introduced myself and Jeff, and said, "Mr. Gibbons, we have a story we think you'll be interested in. We plan to paddle a canoe from New York to Nome, Alaska."

"Jesus," he muttered, the surprise showing in his voice. "You're talking about an inland waterway, a Northwest Passage. Can it be done?"

"Sure," I volunteered. "We've traced the route on maps. It will be 7,000 miles, the longest canoe trip in history. One hundred fifty miles of portages."

Gibbons studied us for a long moment, trying to gauge, I suppose, whether we had the intestinal fortitude to attempt and complete an undertaking of such magnitude. Satisfied, he pounded me on the back, barked, "Great. I've got to have you on my show. You'll do an interview, won't you?"

"Absolutely," I told him.

"From New York to Nome," he repeated, and then reacting to the short amount of time until his live radio program, he said, "Jesus, we have to have a script." He fumbled in his coat pocket, produced a pencil and a piece of folded paper, unfolded it to see how important it was, and wrote New York to Nome on the open side. He asked us to spell our names and we obliged.

"When are you departing?" he wanted to know.

A date popped into my head. "April 25th."

"This year?"

"This year."

"And you are leaving from where?"

"The foot of 42nd Street." I do not know where that came from.

"Great! I love it! From the heart of civilization to the wilds of the North American continent. This will be great. I'll lead the program off with you." Then saying there were a few things he had to attend to he left us, took a seat at the table, practiced his opening remarks. I nudged Jeff. He was speechless.

Gibbons went through his microphone check. The spotlight was on him. For some strange reason I felt like a boxer waiting

12

for the opening bell. Our moment was coming. I nervously wiped my brow with my handkerchief. I saw one lazy puff of white in a windless sky. I knew I never wanted to be an accountant or a salesman or a corporate puppet. I would have gone to college but thought I would be wasting the four years. I wanted to experience life, really experience it. Here we go.

I felt a certain tug of desperation at devoting the next eighteen months of my life working toward a single goal. What was I giving up? My job. But what the heck, I was only making sixteen bucks—eighteen, counting the two Jeff kicked in. Total, I would be losing less than fifteen hundred dollars, with a chance of a much larger return in the long run when the book and movie came out. Most certainly, I would lose Sidney.

Gibbons started and Jeff leaned over to me and whispered, "The Floyd Gibbons Show—I can't believe it!"

Gibbons gave us the high sign. I felt a touch of vertigo but moved instinctively toward the table. He had cut to a commercial. I felt a little fated, and doomed like a soldier about to enter battle. I was afraid my voice would be tight.

As I took a seat at the table my confidence never wavered. And yet the many microphones before us threatened, like the heads of rattlesnakes ready to strike. The knot in my stomach took another twist. I might have felt uneasy but I don't think I ever projected uneasiness. Just before we went on the air, blood flowed back into my veins. I thought to myself that all a man needs to swim is self-confidence. No ordinary human being would ever sink to a depth of more than three feet or so. It is the panic of the moment that gets you in trouble. My mouth was as dry as an overcooked steak.

Gibbons explained to his national radio audience that his program that evening was emanating from New York's Grand Central Palace, the Sportsman Show, and went on to say that he had the distinct pleasure to introduce, "... two strong, young, determined men—Shell Taylor and Jeff Pope. They are about to set off on an expedition to prove once and for all the existence of a Northwest Passage. They will paddle a canoe from the foot of 42nd Street in New York City to Nome, Alaska. These fine young gentlemen are bent on discovering an inland waterway. History will reserve a place for them."

I found myself taking urgent breaths, like someone who has dived too deep. I caught hold. We were in the circle of the spotlight. A few people clapped politely. I could not see them. I blinked several times. A shot of adrenaline hit me. A single drop of sweat rolled over my ribs. It was vitally important to do good. Everything hinged on the performance. Afterward there would be sponsors. That was a cinch. In the darkness beyond, photographers snapped pictures, tiny explosions of light burst like heartbeats. Gibbons welcomed us. I said, "Good evening," and thanked him for having us on. Gibbons began, asking Jeff, "Why do you think you will succeed when so many others have failed?"

"Because we have obtained detailed maps. We have planned every last detail. We are determined and have vowed to go the distance," answered Jeff.

Gibbons asked me to comment on whether the animals we would face in the north country would be of any concern to us. I told him, "No. We are experienced woodsmen." I was speaking of my personal experience. My uncle had taught me survival in the Coast Range of California, techniques that could be used anywhere. I had paddled many a mile in a canoe. Gibbons wanted to know why we were attempting such an expedition and I told him, "Because we will be the first to cross North America by water. No one has ever done that."

Gibbons gave the date we were departing, April 25th, and said we were leaving from the foot of 42nd Street. He reiterated the part about going from the heart of civilization to the wilds of North America. He wished us all the luck in the world. And then it was over.

Jeff and I remained the center of attention. The crowd pressed in and several reporters fired questions at us. We answered easily and basked in the limelight, even signed a few autographs and shook hands with several of the well-wishers.

Outside the Palace, on the street, we went unrecognized. But hell, we were so full of ourselves, the coup we had pulled, it never dawned we were merely faces in the crowd. I was giddy, telling Jeff it was really going to happen. All of a sudden Jeff stopped dead in his tracks, got this completely blank look like he might have been staring through the wide-open gates of heaven or hell, and made an effort to speak. His lips moved, a strained voice quite unlike Jeff's said, "How many were listening?"

"Millions," I shot back, momentarily not seeing the individual people, not seeing Muriel, Sidney, Dad, Mother. The cat was out of the bag. We had kept things quiet up to that point. Now we were absolutely committed.

We started walking again. We were wrapped in private thoughts about how loved ones would take the news. Muriel would probably just laugh and say the expedition sounded like something her crazy brother would do. Dad would not have anything to say, outside of maybe a humph, but Mother would write me a long letter warning of the dangers and imploring I not undertake it. She knew if I started I would finish. Sidney would be mad; her Italian temper would hit the roof, probably not so much because I was going away but that I never shared it with her. I thought enough of her that I should have told her, I suppose.

The last thing Jeff said before we split to go home was, "I hope the hell Bernard Macfadden wasn't listening tonight." He certainly had a way of putting things into perspective.

CHAPTER 3

Monday morning I went through the process of adding columns of numbers, expecting at any instant to be tapped on the shoulder by old man Macfadden and unceremoniously canned. As it turned out, nothing was said, absolutely nothing. By noon I was so cocky I told Jeff we were going to keep the appointment we had made with a reporter from UPI at the height of our glory on Saturday evening. We took a late lunch and met him in his office for what turned out to be more of a lecture than an interview. He invited us to be seated and informed us, "You're biting off an awful big bite. The Far North can be unforgiving."

"We'll make it," I told him with what I hoped had an edge of metallic hardness. "With planning, teamwork and good old redblooded American determination."

"That's well and good," he spoke, "but do me one favor. Before you go any further get hold of a book, *Lure of the Labrador* by Dillion Wallace. It's a story about the back country. It tells it the way it is. Doesn't pull any punches."

I assured him we would read the title he suggested and that satisfied him enough so he could start asking questions and taking notes, things he should have been doing from the beginning.

After work I swung by the library and checked out a copy of *Lure of the Labrador*. It made interesting and entertaining reading. It was about two men, Dillion Wallace and George Hubbard, and the canoe trip they made to the interior of Labrador. They committed a single mistake, took a wrong river, and everything they did after that compounded the mistake. They got bushed, argued and fought. They were lost. Winter caught them. The waterways froze. They ran out of food. Hubbard died. Wallace, by the grace of God, was rescued by Indians.

I am sure the reporter from UPI had our best interests at heart. Maybe he had gotten himself in trouble in the bush at some time, or one of his friends had. He wanted to sober us to the dangers, to the possibility of death. I had already considered that, had thought it through and was willing to put my life on the line to accomplish something unique in history. My lust for adventure was aroused all the more by reading the book. I was ready to leave immediately. But there were a few details to be taken care of. We needed sponsors, money and a canoe.

I gave Jeff *Lure of the Labrador* to read. The next morning we discussed the danger. We would be facing the same risks as Hubbard and Wallace , but we concluded there were inherent hazards in anything. One might get hit by an automobile crossing the street. There were a million ways to die.

The two things we had to have, sponsors and their money, eluded us. We took extra long lunches and met with representatives of advertising and publishing houses. All we got for our effort were variations of the word no. Presidents and general managers, seated in stuffed leather chairs behind massive teak desks, begged off, saying, "We can't afford, at this time, to become involved." Sure, there was a depression going on. I realized that, but there still had to be money dangling on the publishing tree. We could not shake it free and were discouraged as hell. We wasted a lot of time on those men. They had no imagination, no concept of what it was we were attempting. They saw with tunnel vision. I wanted to yell, "Open your eyes!" Of course, it would do no good. They wanted to reserve the chance to publish our book after we got back but they weren't willing to come across with any sponsorship money. I told them we did not play ball without cash up front.

A time or two I got a bit short-tempered, but Christ on a flatcar, we were running out of days. They were slipping past at an alarming rate. The question I kept asking was, how in hell on clerks' salaries were we going to finance this expedition?

And then Bernard Macfadden caught on. He was a big-time publisher and probably heard through the grapevine we were trying to peddle our book. He sent his son-in-law, our boss, Joe Wiegers to talk to us. Wiegers came strolling up like he was God's gift to publishing and demanded to know, "What's this about some crazy scheme the two of you have dreamed up? Is this a lark?"

"No lark," I assured him.

He lit a cigarette and blew a thin line of smoke in my general direction. "Okay," he began, "for your information there are a

17

couple million men standing in line for your jobs. I won't have any trouble replacing you."

His attitude made me mad. "Fire us now if you want, or wait a few days and we'll take care of it for you. Either way, two unemployed men are going to be awful damn happy."

"That's the way it is?" Wiegers was looking directly at Jeff. Jeff stood his ground. "That's the way it is."

Wiegers started to walk away, stopped and whirled around. "How in hell are you going to finance this little adventure? No one is going to pay you beforehand."

On a whim I told him Bernard Macfadden was, and that slowed him. But he came back with, "Mr. Macfadden is not." He let out a huff and this time did march away.

Jeff and I talked it over. We assumed we still had jobs. I told Jeff, "I don't think Wiegers knows what he's talking about. Macfadden would be a natural."

I secretly sensed Bernard Macfadden had sent Wiegers to feel us out. When it came right down to it, he would ask to sponsor us. He published seventeen magazines, mostly pulp, and surely one of them would be the perfect vehicle for installments of our progress. I decided we might as well go for broke and suggested to Jeff we draft a proposal to the old man.

The proposal was drafted on company stationery. We addressed it to Mr. Macfadden. The heading said it all: "By Canoe From New York to Nome, Alaska." In the body we laid out the details of our proposed expedition: "Seven thousand miles through the inland waterways of Canada. A trip never made before. Knowing your admiration for physical endurance and intelligent planning, we want to offer for your suggestions and possible support, the details of this record-breaking trip.

"We are two of your employees in the circulation department, ages 22 and 24, single, both in excellent physical trim, and both with considerable experience in the woods. We have spent a great deal of time planning every detail of the trip and have assembled all data, maps and information necessary. In this matter we have been assisted by the Canadian Department of the Interior, the Hudson's Bay Company, Canadian National Railways, Abercrombie and Fitch, Major Anthony Fiala (Arctic Explorer), the U.S. Geodedic Survey, and many others.

"Briefly, the plan is to leave New York by canoe, thence up the Hudson River through a chain of Canadian lakes and rivers. Approaching winter will necessitate our holing in at Fort Chipewyan, a Hudson's Bay post in northern Alberta. With the arrival of spring thaw we shall continue on to Nome, our destination.

"Our plans call for us to depart New York at the foot of 42nd Street, this April 25th."

The last paragraph we complimented him and gave the pitch. "Your world-wide reputation for interest in physical condition and youthful adventurers convinced us a tie-up with Macfadden Publications would be mutually beneficial. First, because of national publicity through the syndicated articles and planned broadcasts; and second, through possible publication of articles describing the progress of the record-breaking endeavor."

We signed it, put it in an inter-office envelope and gave it to the mail lady to buck upstairs. And then we waited. At first I felt smug knowing the old man had to go for it. We waited more and I slid down the sharp angle of self-doubt. I thought at least he could have the decency one way or the other to get back to us.

Finally Wiegers came to our desks, swaggering and grinning. With great delight he let it be known, "Mr. Macfadden thinks . . ." He paused, playing with us like a cat plays with a mouse, and then went on, ". . . it is extremely dangerous. He is convinced you will kill yourselves and he doesn't want his name linked with failure. He is not going to bankroll your crazy scheme. So forget it."

Wiegers, I could have busted him in half. I ground my teeth. With jaw muscles popped, I tried telling that simpleton, "We're not talking about some C.C. Pyle promotion here. This isn't something we dreamed up on the spur of the moment. This is a serious expedition, of considerable merit."

Wiegers left without firing us. This time I was sure it was an oversight that would soon be corrected. By 4:30 we had still not been given a formal heave-ho. Hell, what did it matter? Let him fire us. What was a few days one way or another? We snuck out early and found a bar.

We sat drinking beer and licking our wounds, bloodied but not yet dead. Macfadden would rue the day he turned us down flat. We would find other sponsors. We had to beat the bushes harder. We had to. But, Jesus, time was running out.

After we numbed ourselves we went for a walk, and as fate would have it, ended up at the foot of 42nd. We leaned on the seawall. Darkness had painted the Hudson an inky black. Unseen waves lapped with the regularity of seconds ticking away. Tugboats chugged back and forth, tooting now and then. A freighter, with all its lights glaring, passed near the end of the pier. I noticed a man on the afterdeck. He was wearing a hat, and the collar on his overcoat was turned up against the wind. He faced the stern, dwelling on the past. I wondered if he were leaving a girl friend or a wife in New York. If he had children he was already missing them. Where was he going? What was his business? I felt sad for his being torn away from loved ones, but at the same time I was happy because, out of sight of the New York skyline, on the high seas and in distant ports, this man was going to find adventure.

My mind jerked back to reality by Jeff's wanting to know, "What are we going to do?" I automatically assumed he was talking about sponsors and told him, "I haven't played the ace in the hole yet. We'll get the money."

"No, I wasn't talking about that. I was remembering what happened to Hubbard and Wallace. They were best friends but they got in the back country and became bushed. Think we'll get bushed?"

I admit he threw me. I needed a second to think and fired a question at him. "What do you think?"

His reply was deliberate. "I don't know. We might. Eighteen months, together in a canoe, is a long time." And then he ricocheted, "Which one of us is going to be boss?"

I was magnanimous in my proclamation. "Neither. We share the work, the accolades, the command." What in hell was I saying? I did not want to share the damned command.

"When we have a disagreement, if we have a disagreement, we will flip a coin to decide." He was getting in on the act.

I knew better. A democracy of two never works. Humans are natural-born competitors, we thrive on competition. Put any two people together and one will come out on top.

We agreed to draw up a list of commandments. Jeff fished a pencil from his coat pocket, licked the tip as was his habit, and wrote on the back of an empty envelope: Number One, "We share command." Two was, "Any disagreement will be settled by a flip of a coin."

I offered commandments so Jeff would not have a monopoly. "We shall divide all work evenly." And, "We shall abide by the laws of cleanliness." I had seen Jeff's apartment.

Jeff proclaimed, "We should never kid the other excessively or play practical jokes." And, "To always be tolerant of the other's viewpoint."

We got to nine commandments and neither could think of another. But Jeff wanted ten. Finally I offered, "Number Ten. That we should faithfully live up to these commandments." And the matter was settled.

20

CHAPTER 4

Muriel was the ace in the hole. When I was being affectionate I called her Mouse, a nickname I had given her years before. She was a good sport, a wonderful sister.

Mouse was several years older than I. I remember how devastating it was when she went away to college, the University of California at Berkeley. Sometimes on weekends she would come to the farm on the Russian River and bring her friends. We would go swimming, and I would impress them by swinging on a rope from the top of a cliff way out over the swimming hole before turning loose and flying. The college boys were all too big and heavy to come off the top of the cliff like I did.

My sister was always very popular. She was a marvelous singer—could play the piano, too. After college she went to New York and developed a night club act that brought her to the attention of the entertainment industry. She married Bob Johnston, also an entertainer, and they moved to Paris where they became the toast of Europe.

Then along came Adele Ryan, heiress to a share of Thomas Fortune Ryan's $135 million, and Bob fell for her. Muriel hit Adele with a half-million dollar breach of promise suit and informed the print media the young heiress had lured her husband away. She sued Bob for divorce and returned to New York.

Before either suit came to trial, Bob was lost in a boating accident on Long Island Sound. Adele settled out of court, giving Muriel somewhere in the neighborhood of forty grand. That was back in 1930. Muriel remarried Wayne Euchner, an arranger and pianist in Don Bester's orchestra. I was sure she still had some of the forty grand, although she and Wayne lived to the hilt. They maintained a lavish apartment at the Parc Vendôme and traveled extensively.

21

I played my ace. At that time Muriel and Wayne were in Montreal putting on a show. Muriel had told me the name of the hotel where they were staying. I sent a telegram, kept it short and sweet. "Mouse STOP Come to New York right now STOP Leaving for Nome Alaska April 25 STOP Paddling canoe."

I guess when she received the telegram she was standing in the hotel lobby with Wayne and Gene Gaudette. Gene was the public relations man with Bester's orchestra and a very knowledgeable man when it came to promotion. Muriel read my telegram. Gene whistled between his teeth and told her she better get down to New York and grab a piece of the action. New York to Nome, he said, had a perfect ring to it. The newsboys would eat it up. He thought it was a tremendous publicity stunt.

Muriel wired back and gave me the time her train would arrive. I met her and we caught a cab to Club 52. The club was smoky and loud from the drinking crowd, and I kicked myself for not making reservations somewhere more sedate. We ordered drinks. Before they arrived, I leaned over so she could hear better and asked what she thought about the expedition. I had been talking non-stop in the cab, telling her details.

"I think it's the most glamorous thing I have ever heard of. I envy you getting to have so much fun. My little brother!" She was brimming with pride. "Where did you come up with the money?"

She was looking right at me when she said it. My silly smile gave me away. I had figured all kinds of clever ways to broach the subject and never had to use them. She mouthed the words, "Shell, you son of a bitch." She had a sense of humor. She told me about Gene Gaudette's telling her to get a piece of the action and his saying there would undoubtedly be deals on a book and a movie.

"See," I told her. "You said he was the best in the business. We've got a winner on our hands. If you want to sponsor us, we'll cut you in for ten percent."

"How much do you need?"

"A few hundred, at least. Enough to get out of town. We can wing it from there," I told her. Good old Mouse, she was coming through. I knew she would.

"This will be strictly a business arrangement?"

"Of course."

"You wouldn't have any objection to having my attorney draw up something?" she asked me. I told her that was the way it should be done and suppressed the urge to whoop. Instead, I gave her a discreet peck on the cheek, thanked her with sincerity.

"You're really leaving on the 25th?" she wanted to know.

"Yep."

"Cutting it kind of thin, weren't you?" She could see right through me. "What if I hadn't gone for it?"

"I knew you would," I told her. She was my ace.

In the cab on the way to Muriel's apartment she wanted to know who we had lined up to handle our publicity. I told her we had been too busy but we needed someone. She gave an exasperated sigh and said, "Publicity is the key. When we get to the apartment I'm going to call Walter Winchell and get the ball rolling. There isn't anyone in the news business with the power of Walter."

Muriel was well-acquainted with New York's upper echelon. And while I took her coat and hung it in the hall closet, she dialed Winchell's private number. I heard her talking. "Hello, Walter, this is Muriel . . . . Well, thank you. I'm calling with a scoop. My little brother . . ." I cringed, ". . . and a friend are taking a canoe from New York to Nome, Alaska. Doesn't it sound fantastic? I'll let you talk to him. Just a minute, I'll put him on." She winked at me, handed me the receiver.

"Hello. This is Shell Taylor."

"Hang on, let me grab a piece of paper." It was Walter Winchell's familiar voice. "Tell me about your trip."

I told him the specifics, told him we were leaving the day after tomorrow. I picked a time, said we were departing from the foot of 42nd Street at 9:00 A.M. on the button. He said he would have a blurb about it in his column. I thanked him and hung up.

Muriel and I sat up for the biggest part of the night reminiscing. It would be our last chance to be together for at least eighteen months. Finally I knew I had to get some sleep and stretched out on the couch. Tomorrow was going to be a big day.

I drifted off for a couple hours and awoke wide awake. I ran downstairs to get a newspaper. It had rained during the night and a trickle of water ran down the gutter where I sat on the curb, flipping through pages till I came to Winchell's column. There it was, a story about us, set apart with a border that made it really stand out. It said, "Good story here, I think; two lads will canoe it from Hudson and 42nd Street. They will paddle to Nome, Alaska, for adventure and photography. Expect it to take 18 months. They are Sheldon Taylor of San Francisco and Geoffrey Pope of Minneapolis."

I called Jeff to let him know and arranged to meet him at Muriel's attorney's office to sign the papers. I think the flurry of activity caught him off guard because he sputtered around and finally said he guessed there wasn't much sense in going to work. How crazy! We were through with Macfadden. The only reason I would go there was to pick up my final check. We had to spend the day buying the grub and gear we needed. And we had to find a canoe.

After we signed the papers and got the money—400 bucks—Jeff and I parted. He was going to Queens to take a look at a canoe with a sail we had found in the classifieds. I was to make the supply purchases. We agreed to meet at Muriel's apartment. She had already caught the train back to Montreal but had told us we could use her apartment because we needed room to double-check everything we were taking.

When I got to the Parc Vendôme I was loaded with packages. I could hardly see where I was going. Somehow the desk clerk recognized me and managed to get a fistful of messages into my hand. I struggled into the elevator and went up to Muriel's floor. The elevator doors opened and I was besieged by a mob of newspapermen and photographers. Once I recovered I acknowledged I was Sheldon Taylor, one of the New York to Nome canoeists. I told them if they would give me a hand while I dug the key out of my pocket I would fix them up with the story of our expedition. But first I had a question for them. "How did you know to come here?" Walter Winchell had given out Muriel's address.

I invited them in and while the photographers had me pose on the floor, surrounded by the gear, reporters—there must have been a dozen of them—fired a barrage of questions at me. I answered brilliantly, I thought, giving them exactly what they needed for a good story.

"Why do you think you can do it?"

"Because we're a couple of young bucks in the prime of life."

"How many miles a day do you have to average?"

"That's a good question," I told him. "We have eighteen months and eighteen months only to complete our expedition. We have to average twenty-six miles a day. If we don't make it to the mouth of the Yukon River by August, the fall winds will trap us and we will never get around the Bering Sea to Nome."

"What will you do in the winter?"

"We plan on reaching Fort Chipewyan before freeze-up. We'll winter there and go out with the ice in the spring."

One by one the photographers and reporters got what they needed and departed. It was down to only a handful when one fellow, a reporter from the Hearst chain, asked a skeptical question. He said, "I've had a great deal of personal experience canoeing the Great Lakes. A wind can come up without warning and last for weeks. What do you do then?"

"I've never seen a wind blow twenty-four hours a day, days on end. Usually at night it will slack off. If we have to, we will travel by night," I answered the skeptic and went on to inform him, "We are purchasing a canoe with a sail and when the wind blows, we will avail ourselves of every opportunity to sail."

Finally it came down to a middle-aged, overweight reporter from the *Times*. He gave the vague impression that once upon a time he might have been a fair high school athlete. He told me, "Do you realize how many people in this world would love to make a trip like this? It's the dream of a lifetime. All the rest of your days you will look back and be proud you had the guts to attempt it. You are going to make it. Damn it all! I wish I were going." He thrust his hand at me and I shook it. I was afraid there for a moment he was going to bawl. His eyes got misty and his facial features distorted as he choked it back. "Good luck," was all he could manage and then he dashed out the door and I was left alone.

I sat on the wooden egg crate. It was a thirty-dozen egg crate, and I had acquired it so we would have some place to stow our grub. I had bought two Canadian packs to store our gear. The gear was scattered around me. It looked out of place in Muriel's posh apartment. I was sitting there basking in my hour of sunshine, but I was like a child on Christmas morning discovering he has already opened his last present. I wanted one more.

There came a sharp rap on the door—another reporter, I thought. Instead, it was Jeff, loaded down as I had been with purchases. Seeing him brought back the warmth I had felt being the center of attention. I helped him with the boxes and filled him in on what had transpired.

We sat there in Muriel's apartment, high above New York, talking and checking things against a check list. Lights came on in offices and apartments and shone like stars through the windows.

Jeff found an American flag I had picked up. "What's this for?" he wanted to know. Patiently I explained it was to be placed on the stern, that it was common for sailing ships to.fly the Stars and Stripes.

We talked about those things we had done and what remained for us to do. Jeff told me all about the canoe he had purchased, said the sail was shot, that a new one would be ready by morning, and that he had taken the liberty of having the seamstress letter "New York to Nome" on the material. "Fantastic," I told him.

Muriel was the one responsible for our starting the expedition. She was staking us, and I asked Jeff if he had any objection to naming the canoe in her honor. He said, "No, of course not." I told him that after he picked it up tomorrow, he should have a painter letter "Muriel" on the bow.

Again there was a rap on the door. This time, to my surprise, there was Joe Wiegers, dressed nattily as usual. I took a step back, invited him in. He was nervous. I told him to have a seat but he remained standing.

"I saw Winchell's column. I have heard the news. You are making quite a splash," he began, paused, and continued. "I was just sort of wondering if you already had an agent lined up to represent you."

"Haven't had time," I informed him.

"You are going to be gone a year and a half, back in the bush. You need someone here to keep you in the news. Right now you are the hottest thing in New York. But no one is going to remember you a year from now."

He blundered on. "Face it, your timing is perfect. Here we are, about to turn the corner on the worst depression of all time. There are no wars. You're doing something everyone else in America would give their right arm to do. You represent that feeling of freedom each of us craves. Who wouldn't like to chuck it all and take off in a canoe? It's a great gimmick. You might have already primed the pump, but you have to have someone in New York with publishing tie-ins. You need me. You send me material and I'll see it gets published. Macfadden will run whatever I tell him to run."

I knew he was not doing this out of the goodness of his heart. "What's in it for you?" I demanded.

"Ten percent. If I can get you $500 for a story I get $50. If you cut a movie deal, I get ten percent."

I was thinking. Thinking. The blurb in Winchell's column or any of the other stories we were going to get did not automatically translate into a book or a movie deal. Wiegers was right. We had to keep our names and the New York to Nome Expedition in the news. I told Wiegers to let Jeff and me talk it over. He went out in the hall.

I told Jeff, "He's right. We have to have someone here keeping the publicity fire burning. He sees the handwriting—there's big money to be made. So what if we have to give him a percentage.

Count Muriel's cut and we still have eighty percent to divide. I don't like Wiegers but I think we have to go with him."

I gave Wiegers the news and he handled it with a smug smile, as if to say, "I knew you would." Jeff was about ready to leave, so I walked them both to the lobby. Wiegers departed. The desk clerk caught my attention, came over quickly. It was "Mr Taylor" and "Mr. Pope." He said there was a free-lance photographer waiting to see us. I said to bring him on.

Jeff and I posed side by side. When the photographer finished, a small girl came over and asked, "Are you famous?" Thrusting a piece of hotel stationery at Jeff, she said her name was Ginger and asked for an autograph.

Jeff turned to me in absolute panic. "What am I supposed to write?" I probably should have told him, "just make it something simple," but it was the end of a hectic day, and I still had a lot of odds and ends to finish before morning. I growled, "Put, 'To my best friend Ginger' and sign your name. You're not writing a goddamn novel."

CHAPTER 5

I packed the gear in the Canadian packs and the grub in the egg crate. An expedition of such importance should not have to pack the food in an egg crate. We deserved better. But we were going and that was all that counted.

It was arranged that Jeff would transport the canoe to the foot of 42nd Street and I would meet him there. I hauled our supplies downstairs and caught a cab. The driver jockeyed through traffic. I closed my eyes and leaned my head back. The hectic strain of the past few days flowed along my spinal column and cascaded off my shoulders. Relief. The adventure was about to begin. It was going to be one hell of an adventure. The excitement was building.

Down along the Hudson the flat gray of morning fog hung close to the water. It would burn off by noon and the sky would be blue and the sun would shine.

What had I forgotten? Oh God, there had been a message from Lowell Thomas, wanting me to return his call. I had meant to. He was too important a man to leave hanging. Wiegers could contact him. Let him start earning his money.

Right after that I remembered cigarettes. The driver stopped while I ran in and grabbed Luckies and Chesterfields. As we came closer to my rendezvous with destiny on 42nd, I wallowed in pure joy. This was my chance to do something, to really make my mark. What a beautiful year and a half it was going to be—us, the canoe, the water. And out there in the future was the promise of fame and fortune. That would be frosting. I could not imagine the fun we would have. The experiences. The challenges we would face. It was going to be so damned fantastic. All I wanted was to get the canoe loaded and get the hell out of New York.

There was a crowd at the foot of 42nd, at least a hundred people. Half were reporters and photographers, the other half from the circulation department of Macfadden. It turned out Wiegers had encouraged them to attend, had given them time off with pay so we would be guaranteed a proper send-off, one that looked good in the media. Jeff was smack dab in the middle, striking a manly pose, leaning nonchalantly on a paddle.

I infiltrated the edge of the crowd before Jeff acknowledged me, saying, "There's the co-commander now." Jesus, that burned me. Co-commander! I felt sucked toward the middle of the circle, the center of attention. Everyone crowded close.

My first look at the canoe and I bristled. Shit, that tub would never make it. It was an ancient Old Town, the type that used to tip over at summer resorts, not a canoe to face the heavy water we would see. If I could have gotten Jeff off to the side I would have given him hell. Him and his damned, decrepit canoe.

I grabbed his shoulder. "Let's go." It was almost nine o'clock and I believe in being prompt. If we said we would leave at nine, then by God, we would. I packed gear to the pier and Jeff piddle-poked around. Finally he grabbed the other end of the canoe and we set it in the water. I almost hated to look for fear the old canvas would leak like a sieve. To my relief, she did not. I set the egg crate in first and then the gear, trying to balance the weight as much as possible.

The only thing good about the canoe, in my opinion, was the name *Muriel* scrolled in fresh white paint. I wished Mouse could have been there. She would read about us in the Montreal news-papers, see us in a Pathé newsreel and be proud. I attached the little American flag to the stern and turned to the crowd. There was Sidney, crying into a handkerchief. I wondered whose hand-kerchief it was. She ran to me, threw her arms around my neck and gave me such an eager and uninhibited kiss that it was difficult to tear away. She whispered in my ear, "Poopsie, I'll be waiting when you get back. Write to me. I promise to write to you." I had given her a map circling all the towns we would be passing through and jotted down the approximate dates.

After we kissed she turned to Jeff and teased him with, "You big galoot, take care of yourself." Jeff held out his hand but she brushed it aside, hugged him and gave him a fleeting smooch on his cheek. Instantly Jeff blushed.

"Goodby, everyone. See you in a couple years," I called. I held *Muriel* as Jeff stepped in and was seated. I checked again for any telltale signs of leaks, saw none, and climbed into the stern. Even though there was no wind, I raised the sail so New York to Nome would be visible.

Above us the crowd lined the pier. Sidney led a group showering us with rose petals. What a send-off! The newsreel boys rolled and photographers snapped pictures.

"Wait," called one of our friends. "You forgot to break a bottle of champagne over the bow." I answered him, "Forget it. Do that and this heap goes to the bottom." Then I called, "Goodby," and dug my paddle in the water. I pulled, and in the flat, muddy water of the Hudson River, there was a tight whirlpool to mark the start of an odyssey.

Jeff tried to paddle, but it seemed he was only fighting me. Under my breath I beseeched him, "Dip, dip, dip. Don't pull so hard. That's better."

WHOOOOOOO-WHOOOOOOO! A shrill, screaming steam whistle blasted us. We had nearly reached the end of the pier without realizing we were on a collision course with the Hoboken ferry. We could have been hit and sunk just as we entered open water. It was with an astonishing, even dazzling, display of teamwork that we were able to stop "Muriel" in her tracks, back her up and thereby save the expedition. The ferry passed so close that mist from her paddle wheel fell on us like rain. Then we were hit by the wake. We went down and straight up; the old, dried-out wood frame creaked and groaned. I dropped to the bottom to lower our center of gravity, but still we rocked leeboard to leeboard, and the mast drew big circles in the sky. From shore, New York to Nome on our sail was probably a blur.

The ferry continued downstream. I resumed my seat. We headed upriver, paddling a circuitous course. I drew a deep breath and allowed it to escape slowly. I looked back and could see the Statue of Liberty, that grand old lady guarding the entrance to the harbor. She had welcomed immigrants for fifty years and now saluted us with her torch, wished us well. I thought about Sidney, could feel the lingering warmth of her kiss, and of course where her body pressed against me. I was going to miss her, and I blew her an imaginary kiss.

It was wonderful to be away! So extraordinarily stirring to be making history. The sun was already burning away the fog. Before long we could strip off our shirts and start getting tanned. It was electrifying to think about the days, weeks, and months in communion with the rivers of North America. They say water is the essence of life and I believed it.

A little later, after we had picked up a light wind and begun to sail, I told Jeff, "Think of those poor devils back at the office, chained to their desks. They'll never know the joy of breaking away. Have we got it made!"

"Yeh, we sure do," said Jeff, without turning around. I needled him just for the fun of it, all in good humor, telling him that was quite a lipper he hung on Sidney.

"She kissed me," he snarled. His neck flushed red.

"Don't get mad. I was just kidding."

"Our commandments say you can't kid, so knock it off."

"Sor-ry," I told him. But nothing could dampen my happiness. I noticed a few rose petals clinging to the gunnel and lying in the bottom of the canoe. I gently set each free. They bobbed over our little wake, and the wind moved them away on their individual courses. They would wash out to sea. Would a princess on a distant shore find one?

We passed under the George Washington bridge. The traffic noise overhead tugged at my heart strings. I was leaving those I held dear. I was severing all ties with the twentieth century to take an ancient form of transportation across the continent. It seemed such an awesome challenge. But we were envied by millions of our countrymen who yearned for a taste of the elusive freedom we would be living. We would accomplish our goal as much for them as for ourselves. How could two guys be so bloody lucky! We had shed the manacles of traditional big city life to live a dream. Terns and gulls kept us company.

We were so ignorant in the beginning, so green, that we set a course right up the middle of the broad Hudson, us in a canoe with hardly any freeboard. We were riding an incoming tide enjoying a tailwind, too; just sailing along, supposing every day was going to be like that.

Along Riverside Drive, Jeff was first to notice what looked like material being waved at us from apartment house windows. I told him it was probably only wash hung to dry. Still, it was intriguing because it seemed nearly every window of every apartment building had wash hanging out. We steered from the Jersey coast and coming near the New York side, it was evident that hundreds—no, thousands—of women were leaning out of windows waving towels and bed sheets at us. Apparently our story and pictures had had an effect. Did they see us as lovers or sons? This final extravagance, as Gibbons had said "from the heart of civilization," was unconditionally the proudest moment of my young life. What a wonderful departure!

31

CHAPTER 6

To reach Nome on schedule, in eighteen months, required our averaging twenty-six miles each day, except for the winter when we would lay over at Fort Chipewyan. From everything I had read, the fall winds generally hit the Bering Sea around the middle of August. Since the final 365 miles, from the mouth of the Yukon River to Nome, would be open sea travel, there was absolutely no margin for error. Twenty-six miles a day, each and every day. If we successfully crossed the continent but failed on the last leg, that would be only slightly better than calling it quits right here. We would prove a Northwest Passage but fail in what we had set out to do: go from New York to Nome.

I established eighteen months as the time limit for the expedition. I had that much of my life to invest, and only that. Then I had to get on with living. Besides, it was highly unlikely the media would hang with us for more than a year and a half—and that was probably stretching it. But if Wiegers did what he was supposed to do . . . .

It turned out to be a beautiful spring day with the temperature pushing seventy degrees. Jeff and I stripped off our shirts. Away from the city, the sun shone brighter and the sky seemed a deeper blue than I remembered.

We sailed and talked. Talked like a couple of kids on a first date. I learned more about Jeff, what he had done, what he thought and felt, and what his dreams were in that day than, quite frankly, I cared to know. He had an irritating habit of dragging out the simplest story and making a full-stage production out of it. He told me about his first bicycle, every lake in Minnesota he had ever been on, and a girl who lived next door while he was growing up. He had never even tried to get in her pants and acted mildly outraged when I asked if he had. He said, "We were good friends."

Jeff and I started trading stories, each trying to top the previous one. To a tiny degree we were competing. But my telling him the story about my professional boxing career (career might be too strong a term--I only had one professional fight) was not to outdo him. It was just a story, a true story of something I had done.

My one professional fight was against Montana Red. He was a veteran fighter with a reputation. I had said, "I'll climb in the ring for twenty bucks." When I told Jeff the story, I even admitted I was scared. No, I said I was uneasy, not scared.

Montana Red was a red-headed cowboy. He had traveled the West Coast putting on boxing exhibitions and had done quite well. The bell rang and he came right at me, trying to knock me out quickly and save having to break a sweat. I covered up, took a pounding. At one point, looking through the ropes, I spotted my father in the crowd; he was eating peanuts, shells and all. After two rounds of this furious, one-sided action, Montana Red punched himself out and was so arm-weary he could barely protect his face. I came to life and was able to do in the last two rounds what he had done in the first two. I lucked out with a draw.

Jeff turned around and said, "You really climbed in the ring with him?" I think it impressed him.

We sailed until late in the afternoon when the wind faltered and then surprised us with a sharp gust. We went from sailing blissfully one moment to fighting for our lives. We should have been keeping an eye peeled; should have recognized the telltale signs of a sudden squall—the time of day, the quick change of wind, the ruffled appearance of the water as the wind came at us. But this day, without previous experience navigating big water, we were oblivious to all warnings. Our mistake was further complicated by the fact that we were shooting up the center of the river instead of hugging one bank or the other. We were in a hell of a fix, a long way out, with the wind whipping the waves into a tempest.

We could not come about as one would with a normal sailing craft because the boom could not pass the upturned bow. We plowed straight ahead, crashing into the waves. Near shore *Muriel* went under. We swam and dragged her on to the beach.

Our situation at that point was more embarrassing than threatening. Much to our chagrin, as we were dumping *Muriel*, a New York state policeman hailed us and called out, "Welcome to Kingsland Point Park." He came up, introduced himself as Jack Reidy, and said we were a mile beyond Tarrytown. Tarrytown was twenty-seven miles from 42nd Street. I had already calculated that. At least we made our average for the day.

Officer Reidy went on, saying, "I heard about you on the radio; your pictures are all over today's newspapers."

"Sorry you had to see us come in like that," I apologized. I felt as though we had let him down. Here we were—the much publicized explorers—and we sink like a couple kids at camp.

But it did not bother him one bit. "Those things happen." Probably to soothe our shame, he commented that the sudden blow was a dangerous situation. "If you hadn't known what you were doing, you would have drowned."

That first night we camped on the floor in Reidy's office. We had a fire going in the stove and all the gear spread around the room drying. It was hot. I lay on my damp blanket, smelling the wet wool. My outermost layer of skin had been cremated from a full day in the sun. It was pink, and my nose and the tip of my ears, exposed by a fresh haircut, were getting bumpy with blisters. Most painful of all were my eyes. The glare of the sun off the water had burned them. Less painful, but more annoying, were my dry and chapped lips. I would endure the irritation as long as I could and then lick them, knowing I was only compounding and worsening the condition. Jeff endured the same.

After our merciless sinking, Jeff and I had very little to say to each other. We slept on the hard wood floor and in the morning were so sore from the floor and our sunburns that Jeff suggested we lay over. I told him, "No way," that we had an average to keep, and we sure as hell were not going to fall behind after one day. "We'll get as many miles as we can," I told him, knowing I would keep pushing until we had the twenty-six.

In a steady downpour we carried the canoe and then our gear and grub to the water's edge. We shoved off. Trying to look on the bright side, I told Jeff that at least we were not going to get sunburned any worse. He grumbled something, half under his breath, that he could not understand why we didn't at least wait for the rainstorm to pass. Piss on him! We had an average to maintain.

We paddled in miserable silence until noon, when we got out of the rain under a railroad bridge and built a big fire. We had sandwiches and tea, two pots of tea, and the warm liquid mixed with honey revived us. I thought it important for Jeff and me to talk out the differences. I explained to him we shared in the blame

34

for sinking *Muriel*. Said we should have been more aware and prepared. "From now on, we stay close to shore, so if a squall kicks up we can duck into a safe harbor." I went on to say I was mad at myself just as much as I was mad at him and that we ought to let bygones be bygones.

Jeff got off his chest what had been gnawing at him, said, "You're not happy with this canoe, are you? You think I made a mistake."

He was right as rain. Our canoe rode the water like a fat duck wallowing through the waves. How in hell could I have faith in her? But I told him, "We'll learn her limitations."

Within the hour we were back on the water. The storm disintegrated and the sun blazed throughout the afternoon. Since there was no wind, we paddled. When the wind finally did decide to blow, it was a head wind and forced us off the water. We started a fire, workers from the Fleischmann's Yeast Company smelled the smoke and came to investigate. They knew all about the expedition and seemed genuinely thrilled to have the opportunity to meet us. We visited with them, smoking their cigarettes since ours were wet. After they returned to work, one of them came back with a paper sack for us filled with a bottle of fresh water, a pound of butter, a tin of tobacco and several New York newspapers that had feature stories about us. We made the cover story on all but one.

We thought we might have to camp on the spot, but a few hours before dark the wind died and we made a run. I was feeling terrible but would never admit it. The combination of sun, wind and rain had dried my skin. My lips and the tips of my ears were cracked and bleeding. Blisters on my nose were breaking. And I had blisters on my hands. My back, neck, shoulders and arms were sore from exertion. I cursed the long months I had allowed myself to be cooped up in New York. I was out of shape and soft.

At one point we passed near a ship at anchor. The crew leaned over the rail and beset us with insults. "New York to Nome canoeists, turn around." The most loquacious hollered, "When your mother goes to search for your bones, the wolves will already have them scattered." I thought that was pretty good, but it bothered Jeff and he shouted at them to go to hell. That was exactly what they wanted, a reaction from us. I kept my head down and paddled. I preferred to put my energy into advancing us than getting mad at a few smart-ass monkeys.

We paddled until darkness sent us to shore on a narrow flat where several fires were burning. I suspected it was a hobo camp.

Not wanting to draw attention to ourselves and too tired to enjoy it anyway, we dispensed with a fire, laid our blankets on the ground and promptly fell into an exhausted sleep.

The black of the night was ruptured by a powerful rumbling and a piercing whistle. I sat straight up. Bearing down on us was a wandering light, an intense eye screaming through the darkness. Train! The fear was all-consuming. I could not move. And only a few feet away, up a short incline, the engine roared past, its awesome power shaking the ground. In the aftermath cars clickety-clacked. Then the train was gone. The lantern in the window of the caboose retreated into the night.

Again I could breath. "My God!" I gasped. Jeff was quiet. "Jeff." My voice was high-pitched and strange. Nothing. I dug for my flashlight, shined it where Jeff had laid down. He was still there. He had slept through it. Jesus Christ, if he could sleep through that, he could sleep through anything. It was a long time before sleep found me. And then I overslept.

When I rolled over the sun was in my eyes. I glanced at my watch. Gads, it was 9:30. I was disappointed in myself because our average was in jeopardy. Jeff had failed me. I had to face it, he would sleep at every opportunity, for as long as I allowed. When I finally did get him going, he wanted to have a big fire, cook breakfast and fiddly-fart around.

"We'll run until noon and then have a fire," I told him, trying to squeeze a few miles out of the morning. If the day followed suit we would get blown off the water for a couple of hours in the afternoon anyway. We could eat then.

The third day of any physical activity to which the body is unaccustomed is always the hardest to endure. If you make it through the third day, things will get easier; your body will begin to harden to the task.

Our third day on the water was a killer. My eyes were so tender I had to squint. My lips were cracked and bleeding and my ears were, too. My nose was peeling horribly. Each repetitious stroke with the paddle made my muscles cry. The small of my back ached. It was painful even to take a deep breath. And my hands were in appalling condition. They were swollen and tender and masked with layers of water blisters that became infiltrated with blood before they finally broke and exposed yet another layer of tender pink skin. Jeff was enduring the same agony as I. He never muttered complaint one. In my eyes, his stock rose considerably. He could take it. We were a good match. In other ways we were miles apart, but physically we were equals.

By the fourth day I was beginning to sense I was over the hump. My body was breaking in. My muscles were less sore; the sunburn was not quite as tender, and my hands had stopped producing blisters. I could more easily endure this level of pain. I was hardening.

We slept one night in a boathouse and another night as the guests of a sea captain who showed us the art of reefing a sail. This was very valuable information because in the future we would be able to trim our sail, have less exposed, and thereby sail in higher wind.

The rhythm of paddling was hypnotic. It sometimes put me in a trance. I would awaken and be several miles from where I last remembered. I was startled from one of these trances as we approached Poughkeepsie.

"Shell! Shell!" It was Mouse. At first I thought I was imagining things. The voice was so loud and strong wafting over the flat water. No one was nearby. Then up in front I spotted two figures on a dock, one of them waving wildly.

"Shell! Over here!"

"Mouse, is that you?" I called, still not positive, but hoping.

"Yes. Hurry up."

I strained to shorten the distance. What if this were a mirage that would suddenly disappear and leave me crestfallen? I was winded, confused, apprehensive--everything I ever knew as an absolute was threatened. There used to be times in the redwoods when I would momentarily get myself turned around. I now had that strange hollow feeling in the pit of my stomach, like that brief instant in the woods when you realize you are lost and think you will be lost forever. But death occurs in the woods only when the lost fail to set a course and stay with it. Simple. Go slow. Retrace your steps. Find something familiar.

Exertion and exposure to the elements had dulled my brain. What else could explain my sentimentality? I was remembering the time Mouse and I lay on our backs under the oak tree in the yard, the time she told me she was going away to sing in New York. I lay there, closed my eyes, but saw a single leaf on a high branch turn lazily in a whisper of wind. The sun burned. The leaf lost the intense green of something living, turned yellow and. let go its handhold. It fell with infinite softness toward my head but missed by several feet. I heard the leaf land in the grass.

"Why do you have to go, Mouse?" I wanted to know.

"I just have to," was her reply.

Mouse was my best friend. When she went away, I missed her

terribly. She was wonderful company, could converse intelligently on any subject from trapping to world affairs. When she left, I pulled more into myself. Now as I paddled to shorten the distance between us, I could sense all my holding back flowing freely toward Mouse.

Thank goodness for my sake I got a grip on my emotions before reaching the dock, or I probably would have started blubbering. More than anything else, my little relapse into the past had been brought on by fatigue. God, it was swell to see her! It had only been days, but it seemed as if it had been a thousand years and many lifetimes.

Muriel was dressed in a conservative gray skirt, but her bright blue puffy blouse fairly shouted. She was wearing a gray hat with a floppy brim and a blue ribbon tied around the crown, exactly the same blue as her blouse. She was a striking woman anywhere, but here on the flat gray of the Hudson she was all the more beautiful. Wayne was with her.

I believe my physical appearance shocked her, even though the bleeding had pretty well stopped and scabs were forming. She hesitated before she pulled me to her in a loving embrace.

"Funny meeting you in a place like this," I told her, trying to inject a little humor into a sentimental scene.

Wayne grabbed my hand and pumped it. I never let on how it hurt. We were on the dock of the Poughkeepsie Yacht Club. Muriel and Wayne, on their way to New York and then Europe, had been waiting since yesterday. They invited us to have dinner with them, an invitation cheerfully accepted.

Jeff and I cleaned up as best we could in the washroom and joined Muriel and Wayne who were sipping cocktails. Over drinks and during the course of a magnificent steak dinner, Muriel withdrew newspaper clippings she had been saving about Jeff and me and read them to us. What a gal! She finished the last clipping as we were partaking of huge pieces of banana cream pie. She concluded by saying, "You're famous," and went on to laud our spirit and resolve. Then she had to say what for a long minute she had been trying to ignore.

"Shell, you're bleeding."

"Where?"

"Your ear."

"So what's new?" I told her and as discreetly as possible in such circumstances, I used my napkin to dab at the blood.

Wayne was impressed by the amount of publicity we had generated. He was around famous people every day, but to him, Jeff and I were something unique—or maybe he wanted to be going with us. Anyway, he treated me like never before. I was no longer a brother-in-law but stood on my own merits. When Mouse slipped off to powder her nose, Wayne told me, "If you need anything, let me know. If you get in a bind and need money, I can wire it." I thought that was awful big of him.

Before we had a chance to get out of there, a newspaper man came to our table and asked if he could have a story. I told him to have a seat, and over a cup of coffee Jeff and I filled him in on our adventures, minus, of course, our sinking.

After he departed I wondered how he knew we were there. I had an inkling Muriel might have telephoned. When I asked her about it, she smiled devilishly. She and Wayne walked us to the dock and gave us a present, a 16mm movie camera and film. We said our goodbys, and it was difficult because I knew I would not see them again until we returned from Nome.

That afternoon we sailed and made a whopping 24 miles in only four hours. The good feelings of the first day when we talked so much returned, and we swapped stories about sports and girls we had known. Just before dark we put in and relaxed around a roaring campfire. Our spirits ran high.

I awoke to a cold fog; my blanket was damp and I was cold. The fire was faintly smoldering and hissing, and the log I had thrown on in the middle of the night was devoured, except for the ends. I heard a loon. At least I thought it was a loon, the cry muffled by the fog. It came from upriver. I took it as a good omen for the day and was nursing the fire with shavings when three deer appeared at the river's edge, not fifty yards away. We stared at each other and then they turned and evaporated into the mist. The fire startled me by springing to life. I placed twigs on the hot spot and then limbs and finally large chunks of wood and warmed my hands over the flame. I put the water on, and while I waited for it to boil, I was forced to move repeatedly to stay out of the smoke that burned my eyes and nostrils.

"Time to roll out," I told Jeff and went down by the river to relieve myself and give Jeff a little privacy. The air was dank with the smells of the river. The sun was a dull ball of yellow strained through fog. A duck called raucously. A fish splashed. I was consumed with satisfaction. How awesomely spectacular the world was! The scabby ears, cracked lips, headwinds, and any other persistent tribulations were a small price to pay for such a glorious way of life.

By nine the curtain of fog had lifted to reveal a sun-drenched day. The Hudson was becoming a real river, taking on the deep greens of the fields that lined her banks and reflecting the blue of the distant Catskills. We skimmed across the surface, leaving a v-shaped wake that disappeared before ever reaching shore. I contemplated the tight swirls in the water made with each dip of the paddle and measured the distance between. In my head I figured we had roughly thirty-seven million feet to reach Nome. I subtracted down until I grew tired of the game and then amused myself with the surroundings and with thoughts of Henry Hudson, for whom the river was named.

From research I had learned Henry Hudson made four attempts to discover the Northwest Passage leading from the Atlantic to the Pacific oceans. He was commissioned by the Dutch East India Company, and on his third try, he entered a harbor and came up the river that was to bear his name. He got as far as the present city of Albany, before running his ship aground and realizing there was very little chance of getting to China in that direction.

The following year, 1610, Hudson made his last attempt, a tragic voyage. This time he swung far to the north and spent a miserable winter iced in on Hudson Bay. The following spring he was cast adrift to die by a crew of mutineers. And so ended the life of Henry Hudson.

It intrigued me to think the only thing separating me from Henry Hudson was about three centuries. In terms of the earth, three centuries was nothing, a drop in the bucket, one grain of sand in the hourglass of time.

Our travel schedule was routine, in a sense almost monotonous, because physically the days were the same: up early, get a fire going, get on the water and paddle until the wind blew us off in the afternoon. Then back to the task of adding a few miles when the wind slackened an hour or two before dark. But the trip was far from drudgery. There was always something new to see, animals grazing in fields, occasionally a rambunctious calf or colt, gulls, terns, ducks, hawks, river traffic, and once we had a fish all but jump aboard. It must have been going after an insect. It actually hit one of the thwarts and bounced out, or we would have had it for dinner.

Jeff and I had adjusted to each other very well. We were working as a team—once we set a course, we seldom varied. We had survived the breaking-in period. Our muscles were hardening, scabs on our lips, nose, and ears were healing, and dark-colored calluses were forming where the deepest blisters had been on the palms of our hands.

We paddled past the Atlas Cement Company plant and were hailed by well-wishers. We waved but did not stop. Jeff wanted to, but the wind was already coming up and I thought we ought to stretch a few extra miles if we could. One of the well-wishers was a girl. Her voice stayed with me for a long time. "New York to Nome canoeists, we love you."

Hugging the eastern shore, we thought we were ready for the big afternoon blow. We would simply duck in before the water got too rough. Our sail was reefed, and we were moving along effortlessly when a wind straight out of the east slammed into us. Instantly the wind and water engaged in an all-out battle. All we could do was turn downwind and attempt to ride it out. The waves increased in size as we progressed into deeper water. *Muriel* reared like a bucking horse with each wave, teetered momentarily at the top before sliding sickeningly into the trough. There was something wild in watching the elements spit, sway, and roar in fury.

I expected us to flip. We were facing for the first time a situation that seemed likely to be more than we could handle. I became quite calm. The feeling creeping over me gradually deadened my thinking but sharpened my wits. Instinctively I felt the next wave growing under us, and I paddled as it swelled. We clung to the downhill side of the wave, riding it as a surfer. Jeff, wide-eyed, looked back, saw my feverish paddling, and he too took up his paddle.

The wind. God made it. God let it get out of hand. God damn it. Can I ride a canoe? Like one was born under my butt. The power of intelligent thought slipped from me. In something less than a hallucination but more than a daydream, I saw Sidney at night before bed, putting lotion on her knees and feet. Blind circles. One false move and prepare to meet thy Maker. If we went under, they would fish our bodies out.

We stayed with it, sometimes losing a wave but always able to catch the next, across the broad Hudson, until we were unceremoniously tossed on a sandy beach. We jumped out just before we touched, dragged *Muriel* above the line of breakers, and collapsed, gasping for air and letting the strain of the exertion seep away. I could taste brassy saliva. Minutes stretched and shapes became objects, taking form like a photograph being developed. A large hawk was circling overhead, casually riding the fierce blow, and I could see mottled gray clouds through its fringed wing tips. I shook my head to clear away dark thoughts. The water had had every opportunity to take us if it had wanted. It could

41

have pulled us down and squeezed the oxygen from our lungs, water seeping into the corners of our bodies, extracting life.

Apparently we were not meant to cash in on Henry Hudson's river. We were allowed to proceed because of our teamwork, and the fact the water did not want us. Not yet.

CHAPTER 7

As *Muriel* was being lifted ten feet to the top of the first lock on Champlain Canal, I reflected on our adventure-bound past week. During that time I witnessed the metamorphosis of a river, as the Hudson changed from a discolored, sluggish tidal pool to a free-flowing river. We had gone from the most populated piece of real estate on the continent to solitude with Mother Nature. And it had been unbelievable, almost mystical, as if we were being reborn.

Put into proper light, the Hudson was nothing more than an hors d'oeuvre, a little something to whet our appetite. It was a training ground, a stretch of water to be used for the sole purpose of hardening us physically, sharpening our skills. This was the foundation on which the entire expedition would be built. The time clock in all of us is different. I am a light sleeper. I can hear a porcupine fart within a mile of me, and at the break of dawn I'm awake and raring to go. Jeff's metabolism was such he could have easily slept in until noon every day of the week. Anyone who is tired all the time isn't at his best physically or mentally. This was a problem we had to resolve. So we talked about it and that helped—some.

Still, each morning I was the first up, getting the fire going, putting on the water to heat, starting breakfast, yelling at Jeff to get up. Poor Jeff would awaken, and his eyes would be swollen and he would be groggy and grumpy. If we had been a man and a woman under such circumstances, the only solutions would have been divorce or murder.

Between us this problem was always in the forefront, and the effects of fatigue and the stress of my always pushing were reflected in an incident that had occurred on the outskirts of Albany.

We were camped on a knoll above the river and awoke to a thick, damp fog. While I cooked breakfast, Jeff hauled "Muriel" and the bulk of our gear to the water's edge. Pancakes were bubbling and eggs ticking on a griddle over a bed of coals when I caught the throaty putt-putt-putt of an outboard motor. I listened as it edged along our side of the river. When it was very close it coughed, sputtered, died.

Frankly I was irked. The pancakes and the eggs were ready. Jeff and the boatman were undoubtedly gossiping. I was about to indulge in a mouth-watering bite, when Jeff appeared from the fog like an actor pushing aside the curtain and coming on stage. I barked at him, "What the hell are you doing?" He never grasped the danger. I tossed my plate on the ground and went racing toward the river, coming off the knoll, jumping side to side like a maniac. I got there just in time. Ahead, in the fog, I saw a shadowy figure lifting our grub box, the egg crate, into a motorboat.

"That's ours," I yelled. The figure immediately set it on the sand. He was dressed in a black hooded raincoat. I stepped in front of him. He was shorter than I, slightly built, with a face dominated by silver gray stubble and loose skin wrinkled grotesquely. His lame excuse was, "I didn't see no one around."

I stood with my hands behind my back, afraid if they were in their normal position one of them might take a poke at the old man. I was so mad the muscles in my buttocks were quivering. My anger was like a billboard; he knew it and got the hell out of there as fast as he could, while he was still in one piece.

Face it, Jeff should have gone back as soon as he heard the motor stop. He should have checked, but he did not. He came on up the hill expecting breakfast. Things were hunky-dory. Bullshit. They were not. And if I had not stopped the old man, he would have stolen us blind, *Muriel* included.

I could see it in the Albany papers, Jeff and me sitting on a park bench with the caption reading, "New York to Nome Canoeists Left High and Dry".

The highlight of the week we spent navigating the Hudson, from my perspective, was that we established the seating arrangement in *Muriel*. We had traded off at first but after that little episode on the outskirts of Albany, I remained in the stern. Jeff accepted it.

The man in the bow is incredibly important, especially in rapids where it is his duty to locate upcoming rocks, and pull and push off. But it is the stern paddler who has the day-to-day control. He sets the course, maintaining or altering direction. Something in my personality made me want to be the stern man, the one setting the course, steering, guiding.

At the upper level of the first lock leading to Lake Champlain, the operator presented us with a letter and instructed us to present it as we advanced through the series of ten locks ahead. He said it would give us preferential treatment, and it did.

The final lock was Whitehall. We were met there by several photographers and reporters from the Associated Press and the Glens Falls Times. Jeff and I visited with the reporters, answered their questions, and then they ran to meet their deadlines.

We entered Lake Champlain. It was as I figured it would be, except much larger, and instead of being blue water like that of California's Lake Tahoe, it was emerald green . . . a reflection of the budding of birch, alder, poplar and the eternal green of spruce and pine that composed the surrounding forest.

Our first camp on Lake Champlain was a sandy beach in a hidden cove. It was ideal, protected from the wind and in a world all its own. Jeff hiked a mile to a farm house and received two quarts of milk and an evening paper for his efforts. We were splashed all over the front page standing beside *Muriel* at Whitehall.

By this point Jeff and I had told and retold our best stories so many times I knew his as well as he did, and he knew mine. My favorite topic was always the Russian River of California. When I was a kid I used to camp out all summer in a tepee. My uncle, Harry H. Sheldon, a famous naturalist, artist, ornithologist, and author, spent long afternoons teaching me about survival: how to dress game, build two-log cooking fires, smoke-cure meat, set snare traps, and blend into the wilds.

Growing up on the Russian River was a tremendous experience. I remember racoons, skunks, owls, and quail messing around my tepee next to the river. That was living.

My heritage was from western pioneering stock. I was fifth-generation Californian. My great-great-grandfather was a 49er. He dug gold, made a fortune, returned to the East and brought the first paper mill around the Horn to the West Coast.

I was born in Berkeley, but we moved to the farm on the Russian River when I was ten. We had a 25-acre apple orchard, and by the time I was thirteen I was doing all the plowing, discing, harrowing, pruning, trimming, and spraying. Dad worked in the paper industry in the city and was home only on weekends. I ran the farm and took my education after riding horseback three miles to a one-room school.

Growing up there had to be better than in the city. I was a happy country kid. One time I remember Dad stretched a cable between trees. He hung a T-bar from it, and I would take it up the hill and come roaring down until I hit the mattress tied to the end tree. What great fun.

Dad also made a Flying Dutchman from a truck axle and a long two-by-twelve with a hole drilled at the absolute center. The two-by-twelve spun easily and fast, and if I could talk one of the neighbor kids into riding the other end, I would get us spinning so we would both be sick. Once I got dizzy, fell off, and the board came around and hit me. I was unconscious for almost an hour.

After high school I thought about going to college. Muriel had. But I figured if I concentrated on gaining knowledge in one particular field, I would be short-changing myself in some other area. I reasoned that by going out into the real world instead of artificial campus life I would receive a more rounded, practical education. As it was, I was an avid reader. I had indulged myself with Darwin's *Origin of Species*, H.G. Wells's *Outline of History*, all fourteen volumes of Elbert Hubard's *Little Journeys*, and the Bible to boot. I was particularly influenced by Edward Gibbon, the author of *The History of the Decline and Fall of the Roman Empire*. He had made the statement that his university career was the "only completely idle interval of my life."

I was not about to throw away four years at college. I joined the company where my father was employed, the Pacific Coast Paper Company, as a salesman. My territory was northern California. I enjoyed the travel, and the money was good. The first year I made $3,600. If they had left me alone I might have stayed, but after three years the company wanted to send me to Portland, Oregon, where I was supposed to learn the paper business from the wheelbarrow up. After educating me in that manner, they would then bring me to San Francisco and make an executive out of me. No thanks. I had seen what the stress of the corporate lifestyle had done to my father, and it was not worth it in my estimation.

I was at the crossroads of my career when Muriel invited me to New York. It was a golden opportunity to continue my education without selling my soul to a corporation. I did not have to think too long or hard. I jumped at the chance, bought a ticket for $33.75, and climbed on a bus headed East.

My first employment was as a barker in front of a theater on 126th Street in the Bronx. I wore an usher's uniform with a cape around my shoulders and stood under a purple spotlight calling,

"Ladies and Gentlemen, you are just in time for . . . blah, blah . . . ." But I intended to make my mark in New York—and now, here, in this canoe, I finally felt I would.

The next morning we took off up Lake Champlain bucking a strong headwind. When we reached Putnam, we put in to rest and resupply ourselves with cigarettes. As far as I could tell, the sum total of the inhabitants of the town were gathered around a potbellied stove in the general store. As we came in they stopped talking to stare at us.

"You're them fellars, ain't ya?" one of them asked. Then I noticed a copy of the Knickerbocker Press lying open to our photograph and story. The man continued, "Them fellars paddlin' clean to Alaska?"

"Yessir, we most certainly are," claimed Jeff proudly. I was not about to open my trap for fear the old man would tell us we were crazy. We had been fighting the wind all morning, and I was in no mood for hecklers and doubters. But the cluster of men around the stove proved to be good sports. We chatted with them about the weather and told of our adventures on the Hudson. They seemed genuinely interested, pleased that we would spend so much time with them. We stayed because it was warm and the wind was continuing to howl. When it tapered off for a moment, we bought cigarettes and made ready to depart. The owner threw in four baked apples and two Hershey bars; all that was asked in return was that we autograph our picture in the newspaper. We did and then bid farewell to our new-found friends, friends we would never lay eyes on again. We returned to the lake to do battle with the wind.

That afternoon the wind blew itself out. At dusk we reached Split Rock. Across the bay we could see the twinkling lights of Essex.

We had a choice. We could follow the eight-mile shoreline of Whallon Bay, the safe route, or take a chance and cut two miles across the mouth of the bay. We weighed the factors. It had been calm for several hours and chances of a wind this late in the evening were minimal. We talked it over and decided to make a run for Essex. That was a stupid, stupid mistake.

We were at the midpoint when a freak storm hit us. The flat water of Lake Champlain was instantly transformed into a nightmare of angry waves. We could have turned our backs to the wind and tried to ride it as we had done on the Hudson but the downwind shore at that point was about seventeen miles. I swung us head on into the wind and yelled at Jeff to keep paddling. We

47

charged the waves like an experienced boxer taking it to a lesser man. We braced ourselves as *Muriel* mounted each succeeding wave, righting herself on the crest and diving into the trough. We took water over the bow and occasionally over the gunnels. It was too dark to see anything but the flying spray and flecks of white foam that danced on top of the waves.

I could feel the blood pounding in my neck and hear it reverberating in my ears. Had we survived the Hudson only to drown in Lake Champlain? Muscles in my back and neck and arms screamed in fiery pain. And then miraculously we were out of it and in calm water. The lights of Essex shimmered like jewels.

We conquered Lake Champlain. At Rouses Point I hiked to the post office while Jeff stood guard over *Muriel*. There were two letters. One was from Wiegers. He wrote that the amount of news coverage we received in New York papers, figured at an advertising rate, translated into thousands of dollars of free publicity. He said to send him the information about our progress and he would have a writer put it into a publishable story.

The other letter was from Muriel. She had included a Paris newspaper picture and story about us. Her note said we had "captured the imagination of the world."

Then we got back on the water for the run across the border. *Muriel* was registered as the first ship of 1936 to enter Canada, and the officer in charge of the customs office wanted the name of the captain. Jeff said, "We share command."

"There can only be one captain," the officer stated dryly.

I waited for Jeff. The expedition had been my idea, I had arranged the financing, I was the driving force that kept us on schedule. I waited. Not a goddamn peep.

Being the magnanimous son-of-a-bitch that I am, I dug in my pocket, pulled out a four-bit piece, and told Jeff to call it. He called heads. The coin turned over and over, hit the floor, did a cartwheel and landed tail-side up. I tucked the lucky coin in my pocket as the officer wrote my name as captain. Jeff was the "Crew of 1".

We left the customs office, hiked to Alexander House, and indulged ourselves with our first shave and first official bath in two weeks. Did we ever feel in the pink.

CHAPTER 8

Montreal was the headquarters of the great fur companies in the late 1700s and early 1800s. What intrigued me was that the traders and trappers had established a water highway across lakes and up and down rivers, stretching from Montreal all the way to the Arctic Ocean. We would be traveling in the shadows of men like Alexander Henry, who pushed the route to the Saskatchewan, Peter Pond, who crossed the Methye Portage and paddled down the Clearwater to the Athabasca, and Alexander Mackenzie, who discovered the river outlet from Great Slave Lake, which he ran to the Arctic Ocean. Up the Rat River and over the Richardson Mountains to the Yukon drainage, we would be blazing our own trail.

I would liked to have stopped in Montreal and nosed around some of the museums, familiarizing myself with the exploits of the explorers, but we did not have time. We were just barely maintaining our twenty-six-mile average as it was.

We made the run from Lake Champlain down the Richelieu River to the St. Lawrence River. Montreal received a cursory, sidelong glance as we kept to the river, paddling against the current and the wind. We swung up the Ottawa River, and almost at once the country changed. The St. Lawrence had been dotted with yachting and rowing clubs and populated with summer homes. But the Ottawa was like taking a giant step away from civilization. There was very little river traffic, an occasional tug pushing a barge or towing a raft of logs; otherwise there were no signs of houses or people. The free-flowing river elbowed its way around hills where waterfalls tumbled over rocky cliffs and mixed their water with the Ottawa.

At one point we heard wild splashing near the bank. I steered

49

a course to investigate and found a mallard with its leg trapped by a partially submerged log. We drew alongside, I reached over, grabbed the duck and wrung his neck. That evening we dined on duck stew.

Our immediate goal on the Ottawa was to reach the Seigniory Club. We had met the Commodore, Harold McMaster, when we had spent a night at the St. Lawrence Yacht Club, near Montreal. We had enjoyed dinner and drinks with him, and he had insisted we be his guests at the Seigniory Club.

The Seigniory Club was a very elite private club located eighty miles west of Montreal and forty-five east of Ottawa. The estate included 104 square miles of woodlands and featured a sprawling log chateau, a developed harbor, golf course, tennis courts, and private cabins. There were miles of trails and some of the best hunting and fishing to be found in the world. The Commodore had told us it was a very nice place, but I was unprepared for its lavish extravagance.

We pulled off the river to the docks of the Seigniory Club. Jeff and I must have looked like the two scruffiest characters ever to come out of the boondocks because an attendant on the dock motioned us away with his arms. We kept coming. The attendant, hands on hips, spraddle-legged like a tough guy, threatened, "You can't come in here. This is a private club. Get."

Just as nice as you please, we turned sideways and bobbed to a stop about two inches from the dock.

"We're guests of Commodore McMaster," I told the fellow.

"Yeh, and I'm FDR," he shot back.

I saw the Commodore coming across the lawn from the log chateau. He came onto the dock, strolled to us, and said, "Gentlemen, welcome to the Seigniory Club." Turning to his employee he instructed, "Jimmy, put the canoe on the dock and carry their things to the Chateau." Then he walked Jeff and me across the manicured lawn toward the massive lodge.

He invited us to dine at his table that night and mentioned he would have clothes sent to our room. He said the chateau had everything available in a small city. There were 200 rooms, all with private baths, and billiard and card rooms, badminton and ping-pong tables, a grill, tavern, ballroom, formal dining hall, library, and a number of stores and service shops. Almost as an afterthought, Commodore McMaster said if we should care for a shave and haircut, he would gladly send a barber to our room. Jeff and I thought that was a great idea and told him so.

We flipped a coin to see who would get first bath. Jeff won

the honor. I stretched out on the bed and fell asleep, I guess, because when Jeff came out of the bathroom he asked who left the clothes. I did not know. Someone had slipped into the room without my knowledge and deposited on the table freshly pressed dark blue flannel pants, white shirts with well-starched collars, and royal blue yachting jackets. Arranged neatly on the floor were polished black shoes.

I took two baths, one to wash the grime off and another purely for pleasure. When I got out, I wrapped a towel around my waist and was just in time for my shave and haircut. Talk about the right way to live!

Jeff waited. We walked down together and had a cocktail in the rotunda. It had the most unusual fireplace I had ever seen, a hexagonal shape sculpted from quarry rock. Twelve-foot logs could be laid in the fireplace. The stone chimney stretched through the high vaulted ceiling. As I stood in my uniform, freshly bathed and with a shave and haircut, I felt like a million bucks.

Jeff went to the bar to get us a couple more drinks. I stood in front of the magnificent fireplace, my thoughts turned to the expedition. Since we had turned west at Montreal, it really seemed we were making progress. The Ottawa River had been a tantalizing swig of the wild country. We had seen eagles and hawks, and songbirds sang for us from the trees and bushes lining the river. Several times we had surprised a deer drinking from the river. It would stand there dripping water off its muzzle as we glided quietly past.

Most of the time Jeff and I paddled in silence. I guess we had talked ourselves out. If one of us saw something unusual, we would wiggle our hips slightly to rock *Muriel* and nod to whatever it was.

It had taken until the Ottawa River for me to shed New York. Gone from my mind were the whine of electric motors and automobile engines, the banging of trash cans, the cough of a wino, the discreet sneeze Sidney practiced. I opened my mind to the silence.

Our adventure was about to begin. The bush country of Canada was before us. The distance did not worry me, and we had detailed maps. What troubled me more than anything was "Muriel." She would never make it. She was too narrow in the beam for big waters ahead. She was a run-down hulk with no beauty, style or grace . . . old, ribs loose, canvas exterior rotting.

Coming up the Ottawa, more than once I caught myself daydreaming, making believe I was one of the voyageurs of the fur brigade era. *Muriel* was not an ugly duck but a beautiful birch-bark canoe that responded to each nuance of my paddle. My spirit mingled with the spirits of the explorers, the traders and trappers. And then I was jerked back into the twentieth century, the Seigniory Club, the absolute lap of luxury.

Jeff returned with the drinks. We sipped Scotch and soda until we were escorted to the formal dining room and seated at the head table with Commodore McMaster. We had an excellent dinner and adjourned to the rotunda where we drank brandy with the Commodore and other guests. They had many questions which we answered, I hope, articulately. The evening was a lot of fun.

After it was over though, as Jeff and I were undressing for bed, we got in a bit of a snit. Jeff said I had hogged the conversation, and I told him if he had anything to say he should have jumped in. From there we digressed to nitpicking. He wanted to know why I did not ease up on him in the mornings, let him wake up at his own pace.

"Because we have an average to maintain," I told him. And then I needled him, asking why he refused to learn to tie a decent bowline or clove hitch. Any horse's ass could.

He lashed back. "Knock it off, Shell. Quit giving me a hard time."

I wanted to say something more, but then it suddenly dawned on me we were acting exactly like Hubbard and Wallace had in *Lure of the Labrador*. I shook my head sadly and told Jeff, "Look at us—we're getting bushed."

Having said that, I forgot about the argument and resolved for the sake of the expedition to try harder. The brandy had made me a bit sentimental. I said the first thing that popped in my mind, told Jeff, "Isn't this the life?" I turned off the light and climbed into bed.

Morning filtered through lacy curtains, and it took a long moment for me to remember where I was. I rose, stretched, pulled back the curtain, and gazed on a dewy rainbow spread across the lawn. A wispy layer of fog clung like gossamer to the river. I shook Jeff's bed and told him to get a move on, we had miles to log.

When I went to pull on my traveling clothes I was astounded. They had been washed and pressed. The Commodore had not risen before we departed, but we left a note thanking him for his most generous hospitality. We loaded *Muriel* and shoved off. Within the hour we were having to fight a storm.

The weather deteriorated, until late in the afternoon we were forced off the water at the lighthouse at Rockland Point. The wood was wet, and I was having a devil of a time getting a fire started when the lighthouse attendant appeared on the cut bank above. He spoke to us in French. Neither Jeff nor I could understand. He waved his arm for us to follow, so we did.

He took us to his living quarters attached to the lighthouse, and we met his wife and family. I could only guess at how many children they had, since they were shy and kept popping up to look at us from behind chairs or the sofa, but I counted at least eight.

The Frenchman's wife served us warm milk and fresh bread. There was no table, so Jeff and I sat on the floor to eat. While we indulged ourselves, the Frenchman dug through a stack of newspapers until he came to the issue with a picture and story about Jeff and me. He showed it to us. It was written in French.

We stayed there, not really wanting to get out in the wind and the rain, until the Frenchman insisted with sign language we spend the night. I had been hoping he would invite us to sleep on the floor, but he pulled back a curtain dividing the room and insisted we should sleep in their bed. I didn't know their normal sleeping arrangements, but I suspected the whole damn family slept in that bed. We told him, "Oh no, we couldn't," but he was adamant. If we refused to sleep in their bed, we would hurt their feelings.

By the time we hauled *Muriel* up the steep bank and got our gear stowed, it was almost dark, and we were ready to turn in. There wasn't much sense in staying up, because we could not carry on any semblance of conversation with the French family, and just sitting staring at each other was dumb.

Jeff and I went behind the curtain and undressed to long johns. I was about to blow out the coal oil lamp when I happened to notice a movement. There were heads lined up like ducks in a shooting gallery across the top of the curtain. The family must have been standing on chairs, the older ones holding the younger, so they could watch the canoeists undress. I recovered enough to bid them good night, and then blew out the lamp.

A more uncomfortable night I have never spent. Bedbugs ate us alive. In the morning we found little red bites all over us. We had to have breakfast with the family. Manners be damned, we itched and scratched and finally escaped the lighthouse only to be caught in a late spring storm, biting cold wind, and spitting snow.

Shell Taylor with his first canoe,
Russian River, California 1916.

Shell Taylor *(left)* and Jeff Pope before
leaving New York.

Shell, Jeff, and *Muriel* leaving from
the foot of 42nd street and the
Hudson River.

Two Get Away From It All, Via N. Y.-to-Nome Canoe

Clerks Take Along Ukulele, Bible and Ten Commandments of Friendship

With only a ukulele and a Bible for recreation, two young men who had grown sick of bookkeeping today took off in a canoe from the Hudson River ferry slip at Forty-second Street on a 6,000-mile trip to Nome, the once golden city of Alaska.

The chief worry of the two young men—Sheldon Taylor and Geoffrey Pope, both twenty-four—was that they might get on each other's nerves during the projected eighteen-month trip through the wilds of the Canadian Northwest.

There will be many, many weary days on the water, up the Hudson, the St. Lawrence, across the Great Lakes until they pass through the Great Divide—and few portages.

Ten Commandments

So before setting out they drew up and provided each other with ten commandments, designed chiefly to prevent one from slugging the other before they reach Nome.

The commandments:

(1) We will decide minor disputes by the flip of a coin.

(2) We shall not try to settle major disputes while fatigued, but shall wait until after meals and rest.

(3) We shall be tolerant of each other's viewpoints in all matters.

(4) We will not permit any annoyance to smolder, but will face our differences intelligently.

(5) The day's work shall be evenly divided.

(6) It shall be "we" in all cases, and not "I."

(7) We resolve not to settle any differences with our fists.

(8) We will not kid each other excessively on any subject.

(9) We will abide by the law of cleanliness.

(10) We promise faithfully to live up to these commandments.

Pope comes from Montreal, Taylor from California. Seven months ago they met in the office of Macfadden Publications here, and almost immediately started planning an escape from their ledgers.

For this purpose they saved $1,000 and rigged up a smart green canoe, seventeen feet long, equipped with a sail.

Fifty boys and girls from the office were there to see them off—and, my, was everybody jealous.

They expect to lay in next winter for seven months at Chipewyan, in Northern Alberta, and continue in the following spring. For the first day they planned a fifty-mile lap that would take them up the Hudson to Bear Mountain, but they will do only twenty-five miles a day thereafter.

Jeff at canal lock on Lake Champlain.

Muriel was the first boat of the 1936 season to enter Canada

Cat. No. 1378

The United States of America

DEPARTMENT OF COMMERCE
BUREAU OF NAVIGATION

CLEARANCE OF VESSEL TO A FOREIGN PORT

[Arts. 148, 149, 150, 152, 153, and 155, Customs Regulations, 1915; Section 4201, Revised Statutes]

District of _St. Lawrence_

Port of _Rouses Point, N.Y._

These are to certify all whom it doth concern:

That _Sheldon P. Taylor_

Master or Commander of the _Muriel_ _(Canoe)_

burden _____ Tons, or thereabouts, mounted with_ _no_

Guns, navigated with _1_ Men.

Canoe built, and bound for _Alaska_

having on board _Personal Effects, Camping Equipment & Food Supplies_

Geoffrey W. Pope

Note:- _These two boys are enroute from New York to Alaska by canoe._

hath here entered and cleared his said vessel, according to law.

Given under our hands and seals, at the Customhouse of _Rouses Point, N.Y._

_____, this _10_ day of _May_

one thousand nine hundred _thirty-six_ , and in the _____
year of the Independence of the United States of America.

_No._

_____ Naval Officer.

John P. Ross
Inspector
U.S. Customs

Collector.

:1—1301

G. Poole of the Canadian National Railways helps Shell and Jeff leave from the Lachine Rowing Club, Montreal. May 13th 1936.

Muriel II and gear purchased from the Arctic Woods Company, Ottawa. Shell *(left)* and Jeff *(right).*

Two pages from the accounts book kept by Shell throughout the journey.

			Phone	10	369.37
			Dinner	105	
			Car fare	20	
			Stamps	30	
		161 13	Cab	07 75	
5/21	cones	40		Truck to Britaine	3 00
	Lunch Dinner	2 00		Wire to Aroprior	35	369.37 / 22.00
5/22	Car fare	15		Chocolate	15	391 37
	Breakfast	85	3.00 SOLD TENT		
	Cab	50	5/26/31 Sugar & cake milk	06
	Cab	75	5/27/31 Fish Rod	2 75
	Wire – NY	93	" Ammunition (1 sort)	1 25
5/23	Pants	115	" Reel	1 25
5/23	Maps	190	5/24/31 Beer	70
5/23	Breakfast	70	" Tampa	20
5/23	Woods Co.		1 doz eggs	
	2 Shirts	6 00	1 Loaf 4 bread	
	2 Sleep. Bags	70 00	1 lt. oil	
	1 Nesmuk	2 75	1 " Sugar	
	1 Can. Pack Sk	3 75	1 " Butter	79
	2 Head nets	1 50	Row boat meat	1 00
	1 Tump line	1 15	35.00 SOLD MURIEL	
	1 Tent	17 50	Cigars	20
	1 Canoe	80 76	5/27/31 Express	6 40
	1 Gun	7 00	Gum	05
	Lunch	85	Cigarettes	10
	Gum	05	Stamps	28

CHAPTER 9

The storm lashed at us, but we kept going, pushing ourselves to exhaustion to reach Ottawa before dark. As we glided toward the Edinburgh Canoe Club of Ottawa, a crowd of people came onto the dock to cheer. They had been following our progress from the reports of river captains and had made plans for us. We were ushered inside and given prime spots to warm ourselves in front of the big fireplace. We were toasted and serenaded with "Jolly Good Fellow," and saluted with a hip-hip-hooray. A uniformed Canadian Mountie presented me with a wire from Muriel and Wayne congratulating us on reaching Ottawa and sending regrets they could not be there to help us celebrate. It dawned on me that this indeed was an achievement. In only one month we had worked our way from New York to Ottawa, accomplishing something few others had ever dreamed of doing. There was a lot more country ahead. But let it wait.

After drinks at the Edinburgh Canoe Club, we were escorted downtown to a banquet in our honor in a limousine that smelled richly of leather. We talked to reporters, posed for pictures with various dignitaries, and were asked to give a speech to the assembly. I told about a few of the happenings along the way, the squall on the Hudson, the storm on Champlain, the bedbugs we picked up at the lighthouse. They laughed and clapped and I thoroughly enjoyed such an appreciative audience. Jeff added his two-bits worth, thanked them and that was about it.

One of the contacts we made was a Mr. Woods, owner of the famous Woods Manufacturing Company that made and sold outdoor gear. He offered to set us up with whatever we needed at his cost. I got him off to one side and told him the canoe we had was never going to make it; I asked him what he would recommend. He suggested a Peterborough canoe, prospector model, seventeen-foot, equipped with a mast step, hole and shoe keel. He said he could get it for us at wholesale. I told him, "Save us one."

We were given complimentary lodging at a downtown hotel. I woke several times during the night hearing the strange sounds of traffic on the street below and overslept as a result. I kicked myself for it, too, because we had a lot to do.

Over breakfast I told Jeff about ordering the new canoe. He acted as though his feelings were hurt, pouted, and wanted to know why I had not consulted him. I told him it was as obvious as the nose on his face we had to do something. The Old Town would never get us to Fort Chipewyan. This was our last chance to pick up a canoe. Sometimes Jeff was so blind to the obvious.

At the Department of Interior we received a cordial welcome. The officer in charge was well acquainted with our expedition and made maps available at no charge. He insisted on writing letters to the various offices along our route, asking their cooperation for anything we might need. He was a hell of a great guy.

We went to RCMP headquarters to apply for a gun permit and did not get to Woods Manufacturing Company until early in the afternoon. By then Mr. Woods had everything he thought we would need ready and waiting for us. Eiderdown sleeping bags with sail-silk covers—the likes of which at Abercrombie and Fitch would have run us well over a hundred bucks—cost us thirty-five dollars. He had pack sacks and fly netting, warm clothes, even a tent that would shelter us in any type of weather. We took it all, including a .22 Savage he sold us for seven bucks. I made arrangements for Muriel to wire him the money.

Our canoe was the greatest thing I had ever seen, a real beauty, wooden-ribbed with an excellent grade of stretched canvas, the ultimate design for big water and heavy loads. Mr. Woods had taken the liberty of having "Muriel" lettered in white on the dark green canvas, just like the first canoe. We disposed of *Muriel I* to a fellow for thirty-five bucks, and I thought we were lucky to get that. I could not wait to try out *Muriel II,* and even though we had only a couple hours of light, we launched. Where the Old Town had been unresponsive and dangerous in rough water, the new gal was a beautiful ballerina skipping from wave top to wave top, dancing my kind of dance, receptive, sensitive, alert, and enthusiastic. Jeff admitted she was a beauty.

A half hour before dark we called it quits to have time to set up the tent. We feasted on rice, peas, bacon, bread and butter, and milk. And then we turned in. The moment I eased into the eiderdown bag, I experienced that same strange awareness I had on the Hudson the morning the deer appeared in the fog. The sacrifices, the physical struggles, were a small price to pay. I drifted off to contented, peaceful sleep and was lost in dreams, until sometime during the night when a storm overtook us. I awoke, and the wind was shaking the tent as an angry dog shakes a stick. We could not travel and were forced to lay over.

It was the next morning, the sky beginning to streak subtle yellow, when the wind dropped off, gusted, and stopped. I rolled out, antsy to get on the water and make up for the lost day. But could I get Jeff to extricate himself from the warmth of his new sleeping bag? Not easily.

Eventually he did manage to pull himself awake enough to stumble over to the fire for a cup of tea. The way he moved, deliberate, like a sleepwalker, got on my nerves. I scowled and told him, "Why don't you snap out of it? Do push-ups, splash cold water on your face. Do something."

"Shut up," he commanded. It was all I could do to maintain my composure. Later in the day, once he was awake, he would probably apologize. God, he was a moody bastard in the mornings!

That day we paddled mostly in silence. The next morning I was shocked awake to find Jeff up first with the fire crackling and the tea water boiling. I told him, "I could get spoiled awfully easy." We both laughed.

We paddled and sailed up the Ottawa River, the river a highway cutting through a deep forest of mixed conifers, cedar, jack pine, some scrubby oak, birch, and short-lived poplar. The eerie cry of a loon drifted and mingled with the environment. Occasionally we would come close enough to see the loon's white spots splashed across its back, and then it would fly ahead and wait for us.

We tried to stop for lunch, but the mosquitoes were so cannibalistic and numerous that we went on. It was very warm and insects of all descriptions were hatching. When we pulled ashore at the end of the day, we had to retreat to the tent to get away from them.

Besides the mosquitoes, there were no-see-ums which tormented us and made red dots on our skin where they bit. And there were deer flies. Deerflies, like large, common houseflies but with a bite to make you yell. They often drew blood. I read somewhere that only the female bites and that the male subsists solely on vegetation. After they mate, the female eats the male. To be more precise, she bites his soft underbelly and draws out his life's blood.

In the morning I could not bring myself to get up and face the insect world humming outside the tent impatiently waiting to dive. I lay in my sleeping bag and enjoyed the evolution of yet another day. The moon was still sending slivers of light over the water when the whistling swans, in a cacophony of whoops and squawks, departed the river. Then Canadian geese joined the symphony; adding to the volume of noise were the quacking of mallards and the trilling whistles of pintails. Not until dawn's first rays touched the surrounding hills did the raucous crows and gulls begin to stir. The metamorphosis from dawn to day was complete.

The morning was liquid and warm. I extricated myself from the bag, started the fire, and threw a handful of green boughs on top to smoke away the mosquitoes. The smoke curled over the fire and the tent, finally seeking an opening in the trees overhead.

The bugs did not bother us on the water. We paddled until late in the afternoon when we came to a timbered spit protruding into the river. We saw a dock and a log cabin sheltered from the prevailing wind by a low rise behind it. A wild rose bush grew beside the door and was blooming hearty, yellow flowers.

Jeff went to see if anyone was home. I stayed with *Muriel* skipping pebbles for the sheer fun of it. I counted nineteen skips, each a little closer, until I lost count. At least nineteen years of good luck.

Two figures started down the well-worn trail from the cabin, Jeff and an Indian. The Indian was bowlegged and slightly hunched, probably from too many hours at the paddle, but still graceful in his movements. He wore soiled jeans, moccasins, and a lightweight flannel shirt. His hair was in long and glossy braids that bounced on his shoulders as he walked. He showed his Indian blood; skin the shade of weathered rawhide, a wide-boned face, hard jaw, tendoned neck, and a strong upper body.

"This is Joe Whiteduck." Jeff made introductions and we shook hands. He had an iron grip.

Joe was probably a couple inches shorter than I, but the way he stood, rigid as a post, he appeared taller. He was the first bona fide, full-blooded Indian we had come across. Standing before me he seemed stiff-starched, hardbound, unyielding, almost to the point of being unfriendly. But I smiled to break the ice, and it did the trick. He invited us to share a pot of tea with him.

The inside of his cabin was like a museum displaying the artifacts of the North. Easily accessible from nails driven into the

logs, hung snowshoes, traps, harpoons, nets, knives, rifles. While
the water heated on the wood stove, I rolled a smoke and passed
paper and tobacco to Joe. We smoked and shot the breeze. In his
clipped English, Joe said he was an Athabasca Cree, educated on
the outside by the white man. He said he lived where he did
because here he could enjoy the best of both worlds. He made his
living hunting, trapping, and fishing, and he took trips to Ottawa
several times a year.

I got him telling stories about the bush and listened intently.
I knew he had faced many challenges and we could learn and
draw on his vast wealth of experience. We shared two full pots
of tea, and I was about to announce we had to be going when Joe
matter-of-factly stated, "Better lay over. Spend the night. Bad
storm. Wouldn't want to get caught out in it. Wind. Trees come
down."

I believed him. We only had a couple hours of travel anyway.
If he said we were in for a hell of a blow, he was probably right.
We hiked to the river, tipped *Muriel* over, tied her on the dock
and packed our grub and gear to the cabin.

Joe cooked dinner, an astonishingly tasty meal of rice mixed
with raisins and bannock. The bannock, he explained, was Indian
bread, the food that fueled man in the bush country. Depending
on the requirements of the individual and the load, each loaf
translated into so many miles of canoe travel. It was my first
introduction to bannock. Jeff said he had tasted it once at a fair
or some doings in Minnesota. I liked the taste and insisted Joe
share with me the art of making good bannock.

He said it was simple: use white or wheat flour, mix with sugar,
salt, and baking powder. Add any kind of grease, bear grease is
best, and water, and mix. The dough went in a hot fry pan, and
the fry pan was set near and tipped toward the fire, propped in
place with a stick. When the top browned, the loaf was flipped
and the other side cooked. The perfect loaf had a hard skin sealing
off the center which remained moist and soft.

We sat up late into the night talking. And the storm hit as Joe
predicted. At first it was a fierce wind, and then the wind slackened
and it rained. Finally we called it quits. Joe blew out the lamp. I
lay in my sleeping bag on the floor listening as Joe eased himself
onto his bunk. The bunk creaked; first one moccasin and then
the other hit the floor. The bunk groaned a final time as Joe
stretched and pulled the blanket over him. Outside, the weather
was an orchestra, rain drumming the roof, wind fluting around
the eaves, and down on the river, the waves kept beat.

By morning the storm had passed, leaving the sky with a fresh coat of blue paint. The sun broke through the woods with long fingers of golden light that glinted off drops of water and splashed a prism of colors through the trees. I kindled the fire and rolled up my sleeves to try making bannock. Joe helped some, telling me as he laced his moccasins not to stir the dough too much, that it was better if there were still lumps in it. My bannock turned out well. In one I had added raisins, and it was the best tasting.

After breakfast our education continued. Joe took us to the dock and showed us how an Indian handles a canoe. He knelt in *Muriel*, back a few feet from mid-center. Under his paddle, *Muriel* became an affectionate girl trying to please. He leaned on his paddle and she turned in a tight circle, first one way and then the other. He took her through her paces. And when he was finished he paddled in—fast. I was afraid Joe had lost his senses and was purposely going to ram Muriel into the dock. But at the very last instant, and all in one motion, he stood, stepped onto the dock and allowed Muriel's forward motion to carry her up, out of the water, and neatly onto his back. It was a slick maneuver that took timing, strength, and practice. He did it so gracefully. I was impressed enough to dig out the movie camera and shoot some footage as he demonstrated again.

Joe showed us the proper way to portage a canoe by strapping paddles to the thwarts for shoulder supports. He also demonstrated a tumpline for both canoes and packs, a strap slung across the forehead to support a load carried on the back. He told us the first portage was in two miles and described the blaze on the tree so we would recognize the spot.

It was difficult paddling away, leaving Joe standing on the dock. Even though we had spent only one night together, I thought of him as a close personal friend. He had taught us a great deal about survival in the bush, things that would make life easier for us in the weeks and months ahead.

CHAPTER 10

We played the back eddies and the slower moving water near shore as we advanced up the Ottawa. We worked hard and sweated freely.

Long before we caught our first glimpse of the rapids, we were made aware of their existence by a low rumble. And as the rumble swelled to an all-consuming roar, I became aware of many conflicting emotions.

Behind us were the interconnected waterways, navigable by ship. It was big water with the inherent dangers of sudden squalls and fierce storms. Ahead were the upper stretches of the Ottawa River and the hump to Lake Huron. I had to think of the expedition in terms of legs; otherwise it was too massive an undertaking. From the Ottawa to Georgian Bay on Lake Huron was one leg, and from there until we left Lake Superior at Grand Portage was another. Short legs all the way across the continent.

The first rapids represented the new world we would be facing. This was the fringe of the bush country. From here on we would be hunting and fishing to sustain ourselves between the scattered settlements and outposts. It was this challenge of pitting myself against the unknown that appealed most to me. Still, I could not help but feel a twinge of apprehension.

The only excuse we had for missing the portage marker was that we were concentrating on reading the current. Joe Whiteduck had said it was clear, a blaze on a towering Sitka spruce. All the same, we missed it, went too far, until the surging current at the foot of the rapids made progress impossible. We took out and scouted around until we located a portage trail leading around the rapid.

The mosquitoes and flies were terrible. There were so many

that the beating of their wings made the air vibrate with a steady hum of background noise. The worst was while portaging; our hands were not free, and the bugs accumulated, which drove us wild. We took turns trading off with "Muriel" and the Canadian pack, until the trail we were following deteriorated to the point where one of us had to go ahead with the ax and chop a path through the underbrush. For two hours we fought the portage, knowing we were not on the right trail. We busted on, and at the head of the rapids we came out on the main portage trail. It was wide enough for a truck. If we had not been so dead tired from fighting the heat and the damnable insects, our stumbling onto the trail might have been humorous. We set the tent, crawled inside, ate bannock, and fell asleep.

I awoke from the nap in an absolute panic; it was daylight and we had an average to maintain. The sun was shining directly on our tent, and it must have been a hundred degrees in there. My muscles were sore from the portage. The insect bites were painful as hell. I moved to wake Jeff. One look and I felt sorry for him, as well as sorry for myself. His face and neck were swollen from bites, and he had scratched himself in his sleep until his face was oozing blood. He went to scratch again and I grabbed his hand, told him to wake up.

"Why?" he questioned groggily.

"Because we have an average to maintain."

"Piss on it."

"Come on. Goddammit, if I can, you can." It was false bravado because I felt like dying. The bugs. How could I face them? How could I continue breathing them into my mouth and nose, feeling them crawl in my ears.

We pushed on, paddling when we could but all too often having to come in, where the insects were, to portage. When it seemed we could stand the irritation no longer, we reached Deux Rivières rapids and a small settlement with a store and a half-dozen log cabins. An old couple who lived there took pity on us and invited us to spend the night with them. We were too exhausted to carry on a conversation. We ate and went to sleep on the floor.

The next day we returned to the miserable conditions. I was feeling sorry for myself, and on one of the portages made a bonehead mistake. I was carrying *Muriel* over my head the way Joe Whiteduck had shown us, when I went to slap a particularly troublesome horsefly. I ended up dropping *Muriel* and cracking two of her ribs. It made me sick. Luckily the cracks were not serious and the canvas not torn. Still, I felt bad.

We reached Mattawa where we would turn away from the Ottawa River. From the size of lettering on the map, I assumed it would be a town of about twenty thousand, but it was a settlement of fewer than two thousand. Jeff lost the flip and stayed with *Muriel.* I hiked to the post office and found several letters waiting. The hot purple envelope was from Sidney. I slit it open with my knife and took a seat in the corner, rather than going outside to share with the bugs.

The stationery, too, was purple, with small flowers in the upper right-hand corner. "Hi, Lover . . . ." She seemed so distant. Could she picture me sitting on the floor of the remote Mattawa post office? Lavender scent . . . I was smelling the aura she walked in. It was Sidney. The air went out of me as surely as if I had been hit low. I missed her, wanted her. I closed my eyes and leaned back against the cool wall. It provided a bulkhead against the flood of emotions.

I remembered the weekend we went to upstate New York. The scene is detailed, the colors crisp and vivid. Sidney, in her bathing suit, standing mid-thigh in the lake. She lifts her black hair off her shoulders. Rivulets of water run over her breasts, down her stomach and thighs. Her legs are lost below the shimmering skin of the ice blue water.

There were quick footfalls on the plank flooring, and I opened my eyes as a young boy ran in, mailed a letter and ran out. He was so alive, in the present. What was I doing sitting, feeling lonesome and thinking of the past? I read the letter.

Sidney said Wiegers shared information we sent him with the entire circulation department. Everyone was completely enthralled with our progress. There was some news about one of her girlfriends getting married and a blurb about her sister having another baby. In the last paragraph she said life was not the same without me and that she truly missed me. "Love and kisses, Sidney."

I took a few deep breaths and rubbed my eyes with the heel of my hands. If I were completely honest with myself, I would admit Sidney was not as important to me as I was making her out to be. Coming up the Hudson I had thought about her often, caught myself longing to touch her, to talk to her; but the farther and farther we got from New York, the less I thought of her. We were no longer connected. Eighteen months was too long for our romance—I could not call it love—to endure. In eighteen months she would find someone else. She was too pretty to sit home alone. By the time I got back she would probably be married and have started a family.

The second letter, forwarded at least five times, was from Mother. It was what I expected. She warned me of the dangers and said she hoped I would come to my senses and call off the expedition. She was wistful and sad. She said Dad had been transferred to Hawaii and that they were moving soon. She wanted me to join them now. Her letter left me more depressed.

I had sent Joe Wiegers a story about the first leg of the expedition and was expecting a check from him, but there was nothing. Since it was late, I decided we would lay over at Mattawa and check the mail when the plane brought it in the next morning. That was fine with Jeff. He never objected to laying over. If it were strictly up to him, we would probably still be sitting in camp on the Hudson.

In the morning there was a letter from Wiegers, a very complimentary letter saying Macfadden would most certainly run the story. Enclosed was a check for ninety bucks. Wiegers had already taken out his ten percent.

Our late start was delayed further by a portage to the Mattawa River. There we were met by a game warden. "Have a permit for that gun?"

"You bet," I told him, hoping he would let things slide rather than make me fish it out of the pack.

"I want to see." I produced it and he squinted at it; then he said, first, it was an invalid permit and second, it had been voided.

"Look, we're in the middle of an expedition. All of this has been taken care of at the RCMP headquarters in Ottawa. Just let us go on our merry way," I told him.

His neck was bowed. "You're going to have to come with me uptown to the office."

"We can't," I shot back. He gave me a wicked smile. I said, "I'll go, and this will all be cleared up with a phone call."

"Naw," he said, "you're both coming with me. You can toss your gear in my pickup or leave it where it is. Suit yourself."

We loaded *Muriel* and our gear and rode to Mattawa. I was burned at the delay, the inconvenience, this authoritarian trying to pull rank. He was taking us in because he had a badge and an ounce of power.

We cooled our heels while he played games through the chain of command. I told him to call the man who had given us the permit, even gave him his name. He did it his way. Six calls later, he was talking to headquarters in Ottawa, and they told him we indeed did have a valid permit. He hung up the phone, turned to us and said, "Well, I guess this time I'll let you go."

"Let us go? They told you we have a valid permit. You aren't letting us go. We have every right to go," I exploded.

"So get out," he said, losing patience.

"You brought us here. You take us back." By God, he had to. Jeff never said word one; he stayed clear and kept his lip buttoned. We got on the water at four o'clock. It was hotter than it had been all day. A horde of mosquitoes clouded the sun and were a constant source of aggravation. By six the first layer of quiet was descending and shadows melted one into another under the heavy foliage of the trees. In this heat nothing mattered except adding miles. I thought about it. We endured the hot, where events had no significance, in order to enjoy the evening cool, which felt like the soothing touch of a woman's hand.

Darkness put an end to our day. We could have battled it another thirty minutes but the mosquitoes were so pesky we had to tie our spare shirts over our faces to keep from sucking them in. As soon as we stopped, we put up the tent in self-defense, and it was such a blessed relief to be inside we didn't go back out to build a fire. We ate bannock again.

I lay in my sleeping bag concentrating on the flight of one lone mosquito circling my head. He landed. I brushed him away, too tired and sleepy to bother slapping at him. It was in this state, haunted by sleep, that the glimmer of something Uncle Harry had told me began to form in my mind. I gave it time.

In the morning I remembered. Uncle Harry had told me pitch and olive oil makes an effective insect repellent. We did not have olive oil, but it was worth taking a chance on the pitch working. I dug around a pine stump and returned to the tent. The outside of the pitch was hard as a rock, but the inside was soft and sticky. I dipped and dabbed and smeared, using a little shaving mirror I had to make sure I applied an even coat.

"What are you doing?" Jeff must have awakened on his own; he had been watching. From his tone of voice it was apparent he thought I had gone off the deep end. I explained about Uncle Harry. To prove the theory, I threw back the flap. The mosquitoes swarmed Jeff.

It was not long before Jeff was painting himself. It did the trick, and we traveled in relative comfort. The mosquitoes would not land, though they still hovered near enough to be irritating.

On Lake Nipissing, at the divide between the Ottawa and the Great Lakes drainage, we were freed from bugs. They would not venture very far into the lake. About the time we made camp, a wind came up, sweeping the insects away, and we spent a blissful few hours. The sun had already set, but the western sky remained yellow. Big blue Lake Nipissing stretched out before us. While Jeff cooked, I used sand and ash to scrub the black pine pitch. I felt like Al Jolson from my face and neck. I paid for it later. My scrubbing irritated my skin so much that I concluded it wasn't worth the pain to occasionally be clean.

Along the south shore we passed fishermen, and I decided to give it a try. Mr. Woods had slipped in several plugs and spoons and some hand line. I tied on a spoon and let it over the stern. It was not out more than a minute before I had a hellacious strike that nearly ripped the line from my hands. I fought the fish, the line cutting the fleshy part of my palm, before I had sense enough to take a hitch around my paddle. Jeff worked us to shore. I played the fish, whooping and hollering, having the time of my life. It turned out to be a thirty-three-and-a-half-inch northern pike. We had all we could eat for dinner and the rest for breakfast.

We entered the French River which drained into Georgian Bay on Lake Huron. At last we were going with the flow of the current instead of bucking it. We flew along ticking off miles like numbers on an odometer. Running our first rapids was an exhilarating experience. Jeff called out boulders just below the surface and fended us off. He did such a fantastic job that after the run I complimented him. He grinned, pleased with himself. It was the first time in weeks I had seen a trace of a smile on his sour puss.

CHAPTER 11

French River tumbled from Lake Nipissing until it was within a few miles of Lake Huron's Georgian Bay. Here the clear water took on a ruddiness, and there were lily pads and the constant splash of fish chasing bugs out of the water. There were many islands with the robust green of pine and spruce, and the delicate pastels of poplar, ash and birch.

Adding to this splash of color, the deep blue of Georgian Bay stretched to infinity in front of us. Despite the richness of the country, I felt there was a hard, bleached, almost bitter quality to the scene. Overhead the brassy sun shone and its image reflected off the water, stinging our eyes and cooking our brains with its double intensity. Flickering columns of heat rose off the flat sheen of the water like shimmering mirages on the desert floor.

We were the only thing moving. There was not so much as a satisfying breath of air to be had, only the oppressive heat. We stripped off our shirts, baked, paddled, and sweated.

We rounded the corner into Key Harbor and were relieved to discover a wind blowing in off Lake Huron. It was a cool wind, strong enough to keep away the insects. That night we slept under the stars. I lay breathing in the fragrance of evergreen, listening to waves lap the sandy beach and frogs making the same low note as a trombone. The Milky Way scattered a path of stars across the black sky and the Northern Lights came out and danced for me. I heard my first wolf then, a lonely, forlorn, far away howling that bounced around in the empty land.

The Northern Lights converged into one corner of the sky, and the color red arranged itself into a peculiar and recognizable shape. A hand formed—a perfect hand with index finger pointing west—and it seemed so real that I felt compelled to awaken Jeff.

He sat partway up, muttered, "It's a hand," then flopped back, promptly submerging himself in his snoring, mindless trance.

In the morning he did not remember my waking him nor the hand. Had it been only a dream? No, I had seen it. I had. I really had. But wait. I was reading too much symbolism into a freak of nature. So it seemed there was a hand. It was the Northern Lights and nothing more.

I forgot about the strange hand and instead concentrated on more easily recognized things, like the fact that it seemed Jeff and I had been plucked from opposite sides of the universe and imprisoned within the slender, bullet-like confines of *Muriel's* slender hull. We traveled in complete and utter silence.

In the quiet of such an awesomely big land, I began to sort through my innermost feelings, began to put the expedition and my own being into some sort of perspective. In New York I had been another nameless face, a bit luckier than most because I had a job paying a subsistence wage. The depression was such a lousy time for a fellow with ambition to try to break in. You marked time, that was all you could do. And then I had dared to dream about the expedition—had taken it upon myself to do something no man before me had done. Here was a worthy goal. New York to Nome by canoe. Eighteen months of my life. What excited me was the doing, pitting myself against the rivers and lakes of the Far North. I was idealistic as hell and never once had so much as a twinge of doubt I would achieve my goal. I would make it. I spent untold hours thinking about the movie that would be made about the expedition, trying to imagine various actors playing me. It was a way of amusing myself, keeping my mind busy while performing repetitious paddling.

We were a week skirting Georgian Bay and the North Channel. At night the wolves and the loons carried on conversations, their calls mixing and tangling, lost and lonesome in this crazy, stark world.

The last morning on that stretch of water I awakened to a fine needle mist hanging over the water. It had rained sporadically throughout the night, with thunder and lightning in the distance. Sometime before dawn the fog had rolled in to shroud us in a lacy curtain. I refused to wait for it to burn off. We had to have a good travel day, make use of every hour of light if we were going to reach Sault Ste. Marie by dark.

"I think we should wait," offered Jeff.

"Well I don't," I retorted. We pushed off into the fog and tried to stay relatively close to shore. The water became shallow and we were forced out. Much to my chagrin we wound up on a mud flat, trapped until the sun finally burned the fog away and showed an escape route.

We did not stop for a break that day but ate bannock as we traveled, and Jeff stuffed himself with bannock. I guess he figured I would keep pushing until we reached Sault Ste. Marie. His gluttony made sense to him perhaps, but not to me. If a wind came up, or a lightning storm forced us off the water we would need the bannock as an emergency backup. Each chunk of the bread he shoved in his mouth only intensified my indignation and resentment.

It was nearly evening before I could look at things objectively and realize how stupidly I was reacting. Jeff eating too much bannock! How damn ridiculous!

Across the channel were the wooded hills of northern Michigan. The good ol' U.S. of A. One small part of me wanted to paddle like a madman, land, and shake hands with the first person I met. But the more sane side told me to plow straight ahead to Sault Ste. Marie, through the lock and into Superior. Lake Superior. We had heard all the horror stories about Lake Superior: we would be killed by lightning, drowned by a sudden squall, windbound for weeks, run out of food and starve. We would be eaten by bears, cougars, wolves. Poppycock! We were veterans. Bring on Superior!

Since it was late when we arrived at Sault Ste. Marie, I suggested we hunt up the newspaper reporter and give him our story before tending our personal needs. That might have been a throwback to when I farmed with a team in California. I had been taught the animals were the most important thing, and the most important thing was taken care of first, even before you tended to your personal needs. Publicity was our key. We had to keep our names in the news, let the public share in our adventure so they would be more likely to want to read a book or see a movie about our exploits. I had lost faith in Wieger's being able to handle the publicity. He should have been pumping the son of a bitch like no tomorrow. I was sending him good reports but he had only managed to sell one story and that was to Macfadden. I was not going through all this, the portages, the bugs, the exhaustion, merely for the fun of it. The romance the expedition was founded on had worn pretty damn thin.

The editor asked for details, wrote like crazy to get all the words. Jeff did not have a hell of a lot to offer. I got the feeling he would rather have been somewhere else, anywhere. He smoked one cigarette after another and was his regular self. After he and I posed for pictures, the editor introduced us around town and bought us a drink. He also made arrangements for us to be guests at the canoe club and insisted we not suffer the indignity of having to portage the lock. He made a telephone call on our behalf. Afterwards, Jeff and I went about the business of stocking for the long haul around the north shore of Superior. Everyone we ran into called us by first name and was friendly. I wished we did not have to leave first thing in the morning, that we could spend a few days, but of course we could not.

With the sky barely giving way to dawn and invisible birds singing in the trees, we found ourselves waved into the lock, a huge lock meant for sea-going vessels. We were gently lifted.

Lake Superior was as flat and reflective as a mirror. The moon flickered over the water. A rooster crowed. The air was chilly on my face and the back of my hands, but with the open canopy I knew the emerging sun would chase the cold away; before it completed its arc, it would tint my skin a deeper shade of brown and burn my eyes until they were dry and irritated.

That morning I was alive, not merely existing. I felt 180 degrees opposite from coming into Sault Ste. Marie. I had pushed myself both mentally and physically to cross the hump from the Ottawa and make the run up Georgian Bay. It's amazing what dinner and a good night's sleep will do for a fellow.

By midmorning a few white puffy clouds marched toward us from the west. A breeze ruffled the inverted world on the gently rocking water, shattering the clouds and sky and the woods into a bright mosaic. The breeze died. The mosaic cleared into a perfect reflection. And again the breeze puffed.

The coast was ruggedly beautiful. Fingers of granite, leftovers from an ice age that gouged and scarred them, ran out into the water. The wilderness began at shoreline and stretched uninterrupted to the tundra and beyond to the ice cap. There was an untamed primitiveness here that I had not sensed before. We were really on our own.

Colors were sharp and powerful. Blue ran the spectrum from the royal blue of the deep water to the soft wash of the reflection of the sky in the shallows. The water was crystal clear. We could see fifty feet down: submerged logs, granite boulders, fish, all magnified by the depth. On shore docile waves rolled gray stones, and it sounded like continuous applause as we sailed along. The breeze sprang from the heart of the lake, and I was thinking this was virgin territory, that we were miles and miles from the nearest human being, when all of a sudden, "Hail, New York to Nome canoeists!" blared from a loudspeaker. I jumped clear off the seat, whipped around, and to my utter amazement there was a yacht, the *Seaforth*, a quarter mile behind in deeper water. I waved my paddle and felt my heart throbbing in my chest, bulging the artery in my neck, still startled by having such a huge ship slipping up on us.

Again the voice reached over the water, "Would you gentlemen do the honor of joining us for a drink?"

I was torn between adding a few easy miles or taking a break. Jeff made up my mind, cupping hands around his mouth and hollering at the top of his lungs that we were coming.

We paddled toward the *Seaforth*. Away from shore the wind was quite brisk, and we rode white caps to the stirring refrains of "The Battle Hymn of the Republic". It was so fabulous and stirring that it bordered on being funny. Several girls were leaning over the railing. I saw them, one blonde in particular. This was a long-distance canoeist's most perfect dream.

We circled *Muriel* to the *Seaforth's* leeward side and climbed the ladder, while the crew winched "Muriel" on deck. Mr. Herman Falk met us. He owned the Pabst Brewery in Milwaukee, and the *Seaforth* was his toy. He introduced us to his guests, including three unattached—as far as I could tell—young ladies. I was particularly impressed by the blonde-haired, blue-eyed beauty wearing white shorts.

Mr. Falk was not interested in my developing an intimate relationship with one of his guests and whisked me away on a tour of the ship, while Jeff went with Captain Anderson to have a look at a set of maps. The *Seaforth* was a floating palace. She was 450 tons and 161 feet from stem to stern. There were staterooms, each with a private bath, a library, and a sun deck everywhere you turned.

We adjourned to a deck out of the wind and over the course of tossing down four or five highballs, Mr. Falk and I became best friends. I was having a hell of a good time with the old gentleman. He had a sense of humor like mine. I told jokes, and he told jokes, and I laughed until my face muscles were actually sore and my stomach was hurting.

The guests located us and insisted on having pictures taken with us. I needed a haircut and my clothes were badly worn, but that only seemed to add to the mystique. When it was the blonde's turn, I asked if she could send me a copy of the print to Muriel's address at the Parc Vendome. Let me show that around when I got back. Life in the wilds?

All too soon our foray into the world of the rich was over. The *Seaforth* swung as close to shore as the captain dared, and Jeff and I prepared to depart. Mr. Falk took his cap off his head, a Milwaukee Yacht Club cap I had previously admired, and gave it to me. He also presented me a pint of rye. I gratefully accepted, told him his cap would make it to Nome but that the rye never would.

They went on yachting. We hunkered down in *Muriel* and fought the waves which had intensified during our stay aboard. After an hour of struggling, we camped on a sandy beach in front of a massive granite cliff. About the time I was slipping into my bedroll, the blonde was probably snuggling between clean sheets. The lapping waves put me to sleep. I dreamed of the blonde and dreamed of Sidney.

In the morning I lay watching the first rays of the sun flicker on the top of the cliff and the swallows darting in and out of crannies. I saw a bald eagle skitter along the edge looking for a meal. And then I was up and going.

That day, at our lunch break, I killed a porcupine that wandered into camp. My uncle Harry had taught me how to dress a porky, and I rolled up my sleeves and went to work. I used my pocketknife to open up the skin on the stomach as you would any animal, making sure not to poke into the body cavity. I split up the inside of the legs and carefully peeled the hide off. After the gutting process, I had a meaty carcass with big hindquarters and small front quarters.

I thought Jeff would be interested in the process, but he was not, although he was very interested in eating the meat after I had cooked it.

The days became like habit. We were up early and would go like hell until the wind blew us off the water. One afternoon we laid over on the lee side of a point. Rather than stay around and watch Jeff catch up on what was supposed to be a daily journal, I headed into the woods. Away from camp I became an Indian, crouching, moving slowly and stealthily. The wind moaned in the tree tops.

Easing around the trunk of a massive Norwegian spruce, I spotted a small buck not more than a hundred feet away; he had not seen me. I used the tree as a shield, lowering myself to the ground. Each time he dropped his head to graze, I stole a few inches. I was downwind, in perfect position.

We danced a slow dance; he grazed toward me, and I crept toward him. Lines intersected. I was so close I could see the hair twitch on his nose, smell the freshness of grass as he chewed, and the warmth of his breath.

It was an amazing sliver of time, and I vaguely sensed our spirits intertwine, mine drawing some of his wildness. He either saw or smelled me, and fear flashed.

"Boo!" I said.

He jumped back, landed stiff-legged, snorted, threw up his white tail and waved it like a flag in surrender as he bounded off. What a startled, Oh shit! kind of look. It was hilarious, and I found myself rolling in the damp forest carpet in hysterics. Once I realized what I was doing, I became self-conscious, in case Jeff should find me and think I was prime material for the funny farm.

I lay there a while more. The wild was in me. I was the deer, the eagle cutting lazy circles in the sky, the loon, the lone wolf howling back in the timber, my voice spilling over the raw desolate land.

The deer reminded me of a time. I was a boy and we had just moved to the farm. The hired man was plowing a field. I was watching him when I spotted a little bird hopping from furrow to furrow. I stalked the bird as I had the deer, waiting for him to drop out of sight, and then rolling over two or three furrows. And finally I reached over the last furrow and grabbed him. His tiny heart fluttered. I could feel it on my fingertips. I suppose he thought I was going to eat him in one quick bite, but I petted his head with my little finger, going in the direction his feathers lay, softly cooing to him, "You're all right. I'm not going to hurt you." And when he was calm I opened my hands, and for the briefest second he hesitated, not believing his good fortune, and then he launched himself into space. Every time I saw one of those birds after that I thought perhaps it was the one I caught and wondered if he remembered me.

I made it to camp at dusk, and from the way Jeff sat hump-shouldered in front of the camp fire, I knew a confrontation was brewing. Sure enough, he growled at me, "Where you been?"

"Out," I told him, thinking as I said it how much it sounded like a husband having to explain a night out with the boys to his demanding wife. I added, "I went for a walk. Why?"

"I was worried, that's why."

It bothered me to have to come in from the wilds where I fit so well into the scheme of things and endure such cantankerousness in camp. Rather than say any more, the two of us had enough sense for the remainder of the evening to keep our traps shut.

Jeff knew the schedule. We had to be up at the crack of dawn to squeeze in as many miles as we could before the wind caught us. But yet I was always the first up, kindling the fire, starting the tea water while the ingrate lay there, until I would tell him, "Sleeping Jesus, it's time you got up." There were times when even that would not work. Then I would come close to losing my patience and might even threaten to physically kick his ass out of the bag. One morning he told me, plain as day, "Go to hell, Shell."

Swear to God, that morning I could have easily left him. I told him to take a flying you-know-what at the moon and started throwing gear into *Muriel*. As I pushed off, he jumped in and flopped in the bow seat.

It was such a pleasant morning with a low mist clinging to the water. How could I stay mad? I started thinking about Jeff's telling me to go to hell and my telling him to take a flying you-know-what, and I got a case of giggles. Jeff turned around and peered at me like a strict schoolteacher assailing the class clown, but within minutes I had him laughing. He would never cut loose in a snorting, honking belly-splitter. He would go ha-ha-ha-ha, the sound emanating from his throat and lacking any semblance of sincerity. But it was a laugh, and it was astonishing what laughter did. It cleared the air like a summer shower. We found ourselves talking.

At first we discussed books we had read, retelling the story and trying to paint the main characters as vividly as possible. After that we got into a discussion of what caused the stock market crash, and still later, we recalled every fact, every scrap of information we had every heard about the world war. I had several good stories about fighting in the trenches and had read everything Hemingway wrote about France and the war.

Jeff had quite a lot to say. He was strongly opinionated. I had to ask myself, if he could be normal like this some of the time, why couldn't he act that way all the time?

The very next morning it was back to the same old thing. I had to kick "Sleeping Jesus" out of the sack. He got up, stumbled around, and on the way to the lake to wash his face, he walked smack dab into the fire. The griddle and the pancakes parted company. The tea fell over and ran into the fire. The fire hissed and burped a cloud of steam and fine ash. I yelled, "You stupid son of a bitch!" I was mad at myself as soon as I said it. Jeff was not responsible for his actions in the morning.

We circled the north shore of Lake Superior, stopping at settlements as we came to them: Michipicoten, Marathon, Coldwell, Jack Fish. Never were they more than a drab collection of scattered log cabins. Port Arthur, built at the site of the Northwest Fur Company's Fort William, was the largest. It was almost a town, with a small business district as a nucleus.

73

It was in Port Arthur that Jeff informed me we were as close to his hometown of Minneapolis as we were going to be. He said he would like to catch a bus home and surprise his mother. He was wistful, homesick.

We had been barely maintaining our average. And if it had not been for me pushing, pushing, pushing, we would not have been in as good shape as we were. We would lose three days if he went. I pulled him up short, "No, you're not going to run off to Mommy."

"Says who?" he bristled. I think he had anticipated this confrontation and planned for it, so I quickly changed my tack.

"Go ahead," I said. "Go. But I've got an average to maintain. If you go, don't bother to come back. I'll get someone else to take your place." I was bluffing.

"Let's flip," he countered.

"Flip my ass," I retorted, pleased with myself because I obviously had the upper hand.

"Damn you, Shell. And damn your average." He breathed rapidly three or four times and plunged ahead. "What happened to all the experiences we were going to enjoy? This is not a race. You're not making it fun anymore."

I did not answer him. His last statement stung me—it hit home. I felt remorseful. "I never meant to take the fun out," I said.

He consoled me. "It was a crazy idea. I'll try to call her instead." He wandered away to find a telephone. I kicked myself for not having made the suggestion to call. I guess I just wasn't thinking.

CHAPTER 12

On the run from Port Arthur to Grand Portage we came across a deserted cabin. We thought it would be a grand camp until I found the carcass of a gray wolf hanging on the door. Magpies and crows, maggots and flies had worked him, stripped away the meat. All that remained was taut hide stretched over a skeleton. It gave me such a start, such an eerie feeling, I refused to camp there and insisted we go on. The waves were kicking up. We fought it for a mile before I felt comfortable to camp.

Grand Portage marked the successful completion of the Great Lakes leg of the expedition. We had survived the temperamental moods of Superior and were ready to tackle the next leg, following the old trail of the fur brigades from Grand Portage, up rivers, down rivers, across small lakes to Lake Winnipeg.

Grand Portage, at the head of the Great Lakes, had once been a great trade center where comers and goers from the East met the adventurers of the West to exchange supplies for furs. The rendezvous was a mix of rich gentlemen, trappers, traders, voyageurs and Indians. Sailing along, with Grand Portage in sight, I took out my log book. One time at the Fifth Avenue Library I had copied down a description of Grand Portage written by Washington Irving in his masterpiece, *Astoria*. I read it to myself:

> Here was a great council hall, as also the banqueting chamber, decorated with Indian arms and accoutrements and the trophies of the fur trade. The house swarmed at this time with traders and voyageurs, some from Montreal bound to the interior posts, some from the interior posts bound to Montreal . . . .
> These grave and weighty councils were alternated by huge

feasts and revels, like some of the feasts described in High-land castles. The tables in the great banqueting-room groaned under the weight of game of all kinds; of venison from the woods, and fish from the lakes, with hunters' delicacies such as buffaloes' tongues and beavers' tails; and various luxuries from Montreal all served up by experienced cooks brought for the purpose. There was no stint of generous wine, for it was a hard-drinking period, a time of loyal toasts, of bac-chanalian songs, and brimming bumpers.

I remembered how I had felt as I copied that, so romantic and naive, thinking it was going to be one endless, fun weekend of canoeing, never envisioning the struggle against the elements: the wind, the waves, the heat, the cold, the bone-weary exhaustion settling on us like the weight of a heavy anvil, the damned insects.

My mind's eye saw Grand Portage as a welcoming spot of international brotherhood, where Scottish partners and French-Canadian trappers and Indians had gathered to eat, drink, sing and dance. The reality for us when we arrived at 3 P.M., dogged by a rolling cloud of mosquitoes and dive-bombing horse flies, was a sloping meadow, infested by insects, and hot as hell. There was no trace that this was the Grand Portage of history books, except for its position on a map. There were no rustic log buildings that had endured the ravishes of time. Not even a sign or a stone marker to give testimony to this being one of the most important places on the route of the fur brigades. I did not even care to prowl around and look for artifacts.

We made a two-mile portage, molested every step of the way by bugs, and then put *Muriel* in a stream so small, its name wasn't even listed on our map, and so shallow, *Muriel* would not float. We pulled her through, slipping on rocks and boulders as we went.

We portaged again to Pigeon River and found it much more to our liking. A picturesque river choked with lilies, it reminded me of Green Valley creek, a tributary of the Russian River. We came across many baby ducks. Some hens would have ten or twelve ducklings swimming with them; others had only two or three. I supposed the northern pike were eating them, gobbling them out of the water with horrible teeth-gnashing bites.

Our work was repetitious: paddle and portage. We added layer upon layer of the concoction of pine pitch and oil but if it dis-couraged the mosquitoes, flies and no-see-ums, it did not prevent them from biting. When our hands were not free on a portage, the bugs accumulated on our necks and especially behind the ears. We scraped away handfuls of bugs and blood and flesh, flicked it on the ground, and kept going. Of course, those areas became infected and were sore. The oppressive heat never let up. During the day we were beaten by the brazen hammer of the sun. At night we simmered.

For sixty-seven miles we fought our way out of Superior's drainage. And when we did top out, on the portage to Northern Light Lake, it was with a sense of relief that we left the insects behind, at least for a short while.

We came in to Gunflint Lodge on Northern Light Lake, looking as absolutely wild as bushmen can look, the concoction of smoky, dirty, sweaty pitch on our faces, hair long, and needing a shave. In spite of it all, we were recognized immediately as the New York-to-Nome canoeists, and people crowded the dock. I was exhausted and would rather have climbed in a hole and pulled the dirt over me, but I politely answered questions. We were always asked the same questions. Is it fun? Have you been catching fish? How far have you come? Why are you doing it? And on and on. We posed with them for pictures and finally, mercifully, were asked to dinner and invited to indulge ourselves in a bath and shave. Jeff and I even gave each other haircuts. We were looking forward to a feast but were sorely disappointed; although the food was very tasty, the proportions were small. As we set to depart, my stomach growled, wanting to know what I had in mind now that the appetizer was taken care of.

The lodge guests came to see us off. Our standard departure was for me to take my seat in the stern while Jeff pushed us off and hopped in. This time he gave *Muriel* a mighty shove, even though he could have merely stepped aboard from the dock. Instead of swinging himself and plopping in the seat as usual, he hung up a foot, landed with his rear end in the seat all right, but his feet, one on one side and one on the other, landed in the water. He was too embarrassed to move. The small crowd thought he had done it on purpose, strictly for their amusement, and clapped and laughed. I paddled away, Jeff's feet dragging and my trying to keep from busting a gut.

Not far from Gunflint Lodge I spotted our first bear. I wiggled *Muriel* to alert Jeff, gave him the sign to be quiet and brought us in trying to put Jeff in the bear's lap. The black bear, intent on eating a fish, suddenly caught our scent, whuffed, and with indiscernible speed crashed through the brush.

July 15 was my birthday. I was stunned to awaken and find Jeff up, and the fire blazing, kicking a shower of sparks into the air. At my elbow was a piece of birch bark on which Jeff had etched with his knife, "Happy Birthday." Beside that a can of beer with a Hershey bar on top. What a magnificent gesture!

"Goddamn, Jeff," I told him, choking on emotion. Sure, it was my birthday. But I was not expecting anything from Jeff. I wondered how long he had been packing the gifts. How many of those portages when our throats cried, actually cried, for moisture, did he think about the beer? And how many times near the end of the day did he want to eat the Hershey bar for the quick energy? I told him, "Thanks a lot, buddy."

I broke the Hershey bar in the middle and gave half to Jeff. The chocolate had melted and solidified numerous times. I closed my eyes to savor the full effects; taste buds tingled with creamy milk chocolate. After that first bite I told Jeff, "What a way to start a day."

I saved the beer until that afternoon when it was hottest. I tied a string around it, and we dragged it in the water until it was as cool as it was going to get. Under the shade of birch trees growing over the water, Jeff and I split swigs.

The beer spurred us to one of our best days ever, forty miles, and I was so happy and ready to celebrate, I broke out the pint of rye given me by Mr. Falk. We each had a drink, followed by river water as a chaser. Almost immediately I felt a warm glow, as the alcohol sent my skin tingling and massaged my tired muscles. The first drink provided such a comfortable, relaxed feeling, sitting there in front of the fire with the moon shimmering on the water, that we had a second drink and then a third, chasing the wonderful feeling. We forgot about dinner, sat drinking and talking, first about what we supposed the country ahead would be like, later reminiscing about the experiences we had already enjoyed, and toward the bottom of the pint, we digressed to swapping stories about girls we had known. Jeff faded early, had the indecency of nodding his head several times during one of my stories, and all at once, in a solid stupor, he got up and staggered to the tent. I was still in a bullshitting mood with no one to talk to. I sat for a while staring into the fire and thinking about Sidney and Mouse, missing them both very much. The melancholy lasted until the last drink. And then I felt like singing, so I sang and my voice sounded deep and resonant in the broad night, the river like an echo chamber, mixing with the croaking frogs, whining insects, the distant whoo-whoo-whoo of an owl. Finally, with the fire dying and the mosquitoes becoming more insistent, I staggered to the tent, lay on top of the bag, Jeff snoring beside me, and promptly fell asleep.

As dawn painted colors in the sky, I awoke with a throbbing headache. I convinced myself I needed another hour's sleep. The next time I awoke, my hangover had gone to my stomach—or rather my stomach shared in it. Queasy and quaking, I crawled from the tent. There on the ground was the empty pint. On closer inspection I discovered a mosquito drowning in the last few drops. I squinted through the neck watching his delirious struggle.

Around the camp our gear was scattered to hell and gone. We were damn lucky that animals had not come in and cleaned us out. Our little toot could have been expensive, very expensive. I reprimanded myself, vowed in the future to act more responsibly. I rekindled the fire and on wobbly legs hiked the short distance to the river. The sun was filtering through the trees and making a cotton mist that hung just above the surface. I washed my face and started feeling better.

In spite of our hangovers, we made it to Rainy Lake that day. The day after, we sailed to Fort Francis, resupplied, and took off down Rainy River, a beautiful stretch with well-maintained farms lining the banks.

We camped on a willow island in the river. After Jeff turned in, I sat listening to the night sounds. A dog's thin bark reached me. He might be very close but the steady rush of the river muffled the noise. A screen door slammed. I shivered and hunched closer to the fire, enduring the plume of smoke until my eyes watered and forced me back. The night was unaccustomedly cool. I shivered again and decided to go to bed, hoping I would float to the still water at the bottom of the day's hard current. I did not. I worried. Wiegers was not living up to his end of the bargain. He was not promoting us. He had skimmed that cream and that was it.

I kicked myself for having been in such a blasted rush to leave New York. We should have taken a couple extra days, lined up a good agent, returned the phone calls. We had made a splash, no doubt about that, but nothing like what it might have been if we had orchestrated it. I was in such a hurry. I had not even bothered to return Lowell Thomas' phone call. If there was one man in America—hell, in the whole world—who could have helped tell our story, it was Lowell Thomas. He was a broadcaster, world traveler and travelogue producer. This expedition was right up his alley. I fell asleep and dreamed that Wiegers met Lowell

Thomas at a party, and Lowell Thomas was saying he wanted to write a book about our exploits. Wiegers told him it was not worth it, that our expedition could be duplicated by a couple of schoolgirls.

I awoke mad at Wiegers and mad at the world. But we got on the river, running with the current, and the nightmare was forgotten. We stopped at a farmhouse and asked to buy milk, but the farmer knew about our expedition and gave us two quarts. He also warned us that a few miles down river we would face the Manitau rapids. He said they were treacherous and should be portaged.

Like so many times before, we found the locals overestimated what they had. The Manitau rapid was nothing. In fact, it was such an easy run that Jeff was absolutely nonchalant, a bump on a log. At one point we took on a bit of water and I yelled at him, but he just turned around and grinned. My smoldering anger erupted. I called him an asshole, and he looked at me with the same surprised expression that he had when I told him to take the flying you-know-what.

Sometimes I couldn't fathom what made Jeff tick. If we upset in rapids, we could lose half our gear, and there was always the potential for a freak accident. One of us might get knocked in the head. An unconscious man drowns. Personally, I did not see myself bowing out in that style.

My name-calling shocked Jeff into the swim of things. Shooting Long Sault Rapid, he was alert and attentive. But as we dropped the last few miles to Lake of the Woods, he was quiet, and I read him as moody again.

Lake of the Woods was advertised as the lake of 10,000 islands and I believed it. Our maps were accurate, and I plotted our course as we zigzagged. The islands were like precious emeralds, solid green with spruce, birch, and poplar, and rimmed by white sandy beaches. We paddled and sailed, making thirty to forty miles a day, until afternoon winds drove us off the water.

We portaged to Winnipeg River and were in some of the most magnificent, unspoiled country man could hope to see. But Jeff (under my breath I called him His Most Royal Moodiness) would paddle with his head down, never seeing the formation of swans busting upriver, or the beaver sliding down the bank and into the river, or the moose that stood knee-deep in water, moss dripping from his antlers. If there is such a thing as mortal sin, it is in not appreciating Mother Nature. We were passing through one of the great frontiers untouched by man. To get Jeff in the swim of

things, to get him involved, I invented a game, competition between us to see who could be first to see various animals. A deer
was worth five points; cow moose, ten; bull moose or bear, fifteen.
This worked. For the first time, Jeff paddled with head up. We
had several tremendous days with point totals going well into
three figures.

We portaged around Slave Dam and were in settled country
again, continually hailed by fishermen or farmers who had read
about us. They offered best wishes and opinions on the twenty
or thirty miles of river with which they were familiar. Invariably,
they warned of an absolutely forbidding stretch of water. They
probably just didn't realize we had already traveled more than
2,000 miles and had gone head to head with bigger water than
the Winnipeg River could throw at us. At times I could hardly
keep from laughing.

Lac du Bonnet was the closest settlement to Winnipeg. We
stored *Muriel* and our gear in a boathouse and caught a bus into
the city. The ride in, ticking off the miles without any effort
(except for the price of the fare), seemed strange. I was accustomed to moving over water at the rate of three or four miles an
hour if we were lucky—not ten times that. And instead of Jeff's
solitary company, there was a bus load of characters: a wild Indian
dressed in buckskins, a civilized Cree Indian in a suit, three wild
kids belonging to a white trapper and his half-breed wife. It was
evidently the kids' first trip into the city. If they weren't bouncing
up and down on the seat, they were glued to the window. What
impressed them most, besides the bus ride itself, were the buildings. As we neared downtown, they craned their necks to see the
tops.

Jeff and I got off and stood on the corner of two busy inter-
secting streets. I felt a little like the trapper's kids, awed by it all.
I had spent too much time in the wilds, with Jeff as my only
companion. We checked into the Albert Hotel. It cost two bucks
but I knew we would get a good night's sleep. After we had a bath
and put on our change of clothes, I suggested we grab a bite and
take in a movie. We saw *Fury* with Spencer Tracy and Sylvia Sydney, and I realized what I saw on the screen was not the real
world. The city outside was not the real world. To me, the only
true existence was the bush, *Muriel,* the constant accumulation of
miles. In the city you relied on someone to feed you, clean up
after you, entertain you. In the bush you relied on yourself and
your partner, nothing more.

We started the morning with a big breakfast followed by hair-

81

cuts and shaves before venturing to the post office. We had a pile of mail waiting and took it out on the lawn to read. The sun filtered through the trees and dappled the grass but the air was foul with the smell of city life. I could never shake the feeling that each breath I drew had already been breathed by someone else.

One of my letters was from Sidney, a single paragraph on off-pink stationery that smelled of skunk weed. I supposed violets were intended. Her disconcerting note read: "Dear Poopsie, The letter I received from you this noon was like a gust of fresh wind blowing into my world. It blew around in my conventional life and departed, leaving all my feelings and emotions askew. Perhaps I am fanciful, or restless, or merely want a change from missing you." It was signed, "Love you as always, Sidney." There was a P.S. "You may be beyond my reach, beyond the realm of my existence, but you will forever be in my dreams."

She was so insulated. She had the extra time to organize her thoughts—she could recline in her living room on a hot summer evening, with the window open and the fan going, and compose perfect prose—but her life still spun in endless circles of weekends and Monday mornings. I pitied her.

Reading between the lines, I realized Sidney had left me. She did not know it yet, but she had. She had gone through her period of mourning and now she wanted to get on with life. It may sound conceited to say, but I had worked her out of my system much faster than she could work me out of hers. I was facing new challenges, adding miles, and fighting insects, until I did not have the strength to think any more about Sidney and the life we might have had together. It would take her longer to forget me because I was a part of the things she did and saw every day. She was still passing the desk where I sat, or a restaurant where we ate.

Examining my feelings, I decided there was not much sense in her holding onto the past. I was no longer the clerk she knew, walking down Broadway. For that matter I was no longer my sister's little brother, the kid from California with big ideas and the gift for talking your arm off. I was my own man. The rigors of the expedition had hardened me, changed me. Before, in New York, I was cocky. I believed, if given the chance, I would succeed. Now I was positive of it. I had seized opportunity, and I was not about to let it go. I was determined: Nome next year. I had endured the fatigue, the craziness caused by swarming insects, had conquered every obstacle—and succeeded—because I had the sheer will, the desire to triumph.

We walked on sidewalks from the post office to the RCMP

headquarters. I explained to the secretary what we needed, asked whom we should talk to. She rang Inspector Brown. Fifteen minutes later we were led to his office.

Inspector Brown was six feet, six inches tall, at least. His well-trimmed mustache was graying, he had a military bearing and the good looks of Clark Gable. I explained the details of our expedition.

His first question was, "Can you survive a year in the bush?"

I sat straight in the high-back chair, looked him right in the eye and told him, "We've survived this far."

"Lad, the real bush country starts north of here," he instructed as if he were a teacher. "What will you eat?"

"We have a .22 and we're crack shots with it," offered Jeff. Inspector Brown leaned back in his swivel chair.

"How will you kill a moose or a caribou with a .22?"

I knew he was baiting us. "We have no need to kill a moose or a caribou. It would be foolish. In the first place, we would have no means to keep the meat except to jerk it, and that would steal travel time. We will survive on small game—fish, ducks, muskrat, porcupine."

Apparently my words, or the conviction with which I said them, impressed the inspector because he rolled out the red carpet for us. In short order, we had maps that showed us the way from Winnipeg to the Rat River. Only one section was missing, and that was a hundred miles or so around Methye portage. I was not concerned; we could wing it.

Later I went to a dentist who filled three cavities, while Jeff visited a doctor. He had contracted an irritating case of poison ivy on his feet that was driving him insane. And his constant scratching was irritating as hell to me. I sincerely hoped the doctor could fix him up, as much for my sake as his.

Chapter 13

On the run below Lac du Bonnet we had to portage Pine Falls. I goofed, walked away without the ax. It was not until we were sailing on Lake Winnipeg that a vision came to me and I could clearly see the ax leaned against the rock where I left it.

We made it to Fort Alexander at dusk where we located a flat spot and threw our bags on the ground. That night it was just too much trouble to put up the tent. We sat for a moment enjoying a smoke and watching the moon emerge, sending its flickering reflection across the rippled water. A gust of wind strained through the trees and made the hills moan. There was a hint in the air that the earth was hurrying on toward other weather; the heat of summer was drawing to a close. We finished our cigarettes, pulled the sail over us to keep away the mosquitoes, and slept.

In the morning, while Jeff cooked breakfast, I hiked to the Hudson's Bay post to purchase an ax. The chap on duty was a talker. He told me the U.S. had taken charge of the Olympic Games in Berlin on the strength of Jesse Owens's four gold medals. He was so knowledgeable about current affairs, I asked him how he kept up. He said he could pick up stations on his radio from as far away as Chicago, or even New York.

By the time I bought the ax and caught up on all the worldly happenings, Jeff had *Muriel* loaded and ready to go and was having a patient smoke. We got on the water, but after an hour a blustery crosswind kicked up. For three miles we fought rolling combers before calling it quits, putting in near an Indian village of tents and tarpaper shacks. I spent time lounging in the tent, writing in my log book while Jeff hiked to the village and rented two large tubs for ten cents. He brought them to camp and did the wash—my clothes included, which was gratefully appreciated.

We were windbound until late in the afternoon, when the storm blew itself out. The waves remained high and the water milky with silt. This made the paddles slippery, a dangerous situation bucking big waves as we were. But given time the lake flattened out.

When I caught my first whiff of smoke I thought I must be imagining things. Before long smoke was quite evident, irritating our eyes and tickling our throats until we coughed. A blanket of thick, gray smoke rolled over the lake like a heavy wool blanket. A forest fire was coming our way, and there was nothing to stop it short of the lake. Jeff and I discussed our options; we could backtrack until we were sure we were below the fire and make camp, or we could go on.

We went on. A plump red moon emerged to cast an eerie, bloody light. The world was quiet except for the gentle slap of the dying waves and the rhythmic dipping of our paddles.

The front was eight miles wide. When we did pop out, the moon bathed us in dazzling white. We could have traveled all night but we were tired, and when we were a safe distance above the fire, we swung ashore.

In the morning, smoke still rolled out in a dirty brown layer over the water. We turned our backs to it and continued north.

Signs of human habitation became few and far between. Occasionally we passed an Indian village, and the dogs would howl. The unchained ones would come to the edge of the water to call their challenge. The comment Inspector Brown made about the real bush country starting north of Winnipeg came to mind. He was right. We had gone through uninhabited territory before, but there was always a city at the far end. This time there was nothing.

Charley lived on a small island with a pack of howling huskies. As we passed he waved his arms for us to come ashore. He was a grizzled old bachelor, a fisherman, originally from Ohio. We talked a while and he invited us to take a tour of his island. We wandered along, making our way through his dogs that were chained and staked every fifty feet or so. Some leaped in the air, going crazy, wanting to be petted and shown affection. Others stood stiff-legged with hackles raised, growling and showing teeth. They were mixed breeds—mostly husky, police dog, and wolfhound, with the remainder being God only knows what. The whole area where they were staked was lousy with flies attracted by mounds of stinking scat. As we came to certain dogs Charley stopped and told stories about them without regard to time or smell.

"They all ain't my dogs," he confided. His rough hand rearranged a filthy baseball cap on his head. He tugged at the bill. "The Indians, they don't know how to care for dogs. In the fall I take in a few extras to get 'em into running shape. See, I fatten 'em up a bit."

Of course, we had to share a pot of tea with the old boy or face insulting him, and his cabin was as disgusting and nauseating as I was afraid it would be. He had a cat that apparently had never been outside, and the shack stunk from him. Sitting around indiscriminately were soup cans filled to overflowing with rancid grease. The windowsills were piled inches deep with the accumulated bodies of flies and mosquitoes. I offered to get our cups and ducked outside, as much for a breath of fresh air as to have clean cups to drink from. The dogs howled and carried on until I returned inside.

Heading north from Charley's for several hundred miles we saw only two summer villages where the Indians were living in tents, and not a single substantial building until the mouth of Warpath River. There we saw a picturesque log cabin, smoke drifting from the chimney, and eleven huskies chained to a log out front. Strangest thing, they sat on their haunches and never howled or anything. It was like they were stone decorations. But they were alive and swung their heads to watch us as we brought "Muriel" in to the sandy beach. Though they were chained, their quietness was so peculiar I didn't trust them, and apparently neither did Jeff. Rather than step ashore, he hollered "Wahoo" a couple of times.

The cabin door was flung open and an old fellow—he made Charley look like a kid—stood on the top step, squinting, tugging at suspenders, trying to get them over his shoulders. He had a shock of white hair sticking straight up. Evidently we had awakened him from a nap. His vision cleared enough for him to spot us; then he scrambled down the stairs and down the bank like a crab on fire. He waded right out into the water and grabbed hold of *Muriel*.

"Come on," he told us, his eyes flashing wildly, "have a spot of tea with me."

It turned out he was every bit as crazy as first impression would indicate—he was crazy with loneliness. He had not seen another white man since way last spring when he went to Winnipeg. His name was John. We had just taken our first sip of tea when he wanted to know, "Et yet?" And without waiting for an answer, he jumped up, called for us to follow, led the way to his icehouse. He called it his icehouse but it was actually a cellar with a sod roof.

"This is caribou," he said pulling a discolored quarter of meat from a strawpile on the floor.

John cooked and we visited. My initial impression of caribou was that it was undoubtedly the tenderest, sweetest, most succulent meat God ever created. I told John so, and it pleased him; he had introduced us to the staple of the North.

After dinner John insisted he put on a show of his shooting ability. He set a bottle on a stump a good hundred yards out and with his first shot blew it into oblivion. After that he made a tin can dance. Then he allowed Jeff and me to have a go at it, but we couldn't have hit a tin shed, the sights being set to John's vision.

I had cooked bannock the day before, and as we departed I gave John a loaf to repay him for his kindness. He told us to wait, ran to the icehouse, grabbed the quarter of caribou we had worked on, wrapped it with damp burlap, and laid it in the bottom of "Muriel." We gave him heartfelt thanks, bid the poor lonesome bastard adieu, dipped paddles, and as we moved away I could hear him back there howling, "Stay the night! Stay the night!"

The next day I shot at a duck with the .22 but only winged him. We had to run him down, and Jeff wrung his neck. That night we cooked a delicious duck and caribou stew, the likes of which you could never duplicate in the fanciest restaurant. The taste included campfire smoke and the spice of the vast land: the moodiness of the lake, the strength of the timbered ridges, and the uncertainty of the boggy muskeg.

CHAPTER 14

The settlement of Grand Rapids marked the head of Lake Winnipeg and the end of our big water travels for the year. From there we would be ascending and descending streams and creeks and crossing small lakes as we hopscotched northern Saskatchewan to our planned wintering quarters at Fort Chipewyan on Lake Athabasca. Covering miles now would be crucial to beat the threat of an early freeze-up locking the Northland in a deadly grip.

A dozen Indians sat on the dock at Grand Rapids; one whittled a stick, and the others watched him or stared off into blue yonder. They made no sign of seeing us. It crossed my mind to play their silly little game, but in the end I treated them civilly, greeting them with an arms-length hello. We pulled *Muriel* onto the beach and hiked to the store where we told the clerk, an old spinster, what we needed in the way of supplies. As she filled our order, one of the Indians who had been lounging on the dock stuck his head in the doorway and said, "Dogs in canoe." Jeff and I sprinted to the dock, chased the damn dogs out of *Muriel*. I caught up with one poor hungry devil with his head in our stew pot, gave him a kick, and sent him sprawling.

The Indians took in the entire episode as if it were acted out for their benefit. I did not know what to do, to give them hell for not keeping the dogs away, or thank them for coming and getting us. I said nothing.

From Lake Winnipeg to the Saskatchewan River was a three and one-half mile portage bridged by a tramway. The Hudson's Bay Company installed it during their fur-trading heyday. When they pulled out, they gave the tram to Grand Rapids.

We had a devil of a time finding any of the lazy locals who would agree to haul us over the portage. Finally we found one

Indian with a swayback pony. We loaded *Muriel* and our gear and grub on the tram car and hitched the pony to it. It was such a novel way to portage, I dug out the movie camera and shot some footage. I should never have done it because the Indian assumed if we had a movie camera we had money, and at the halfway point announced the price of the portage was two dollars, not the one dollar we had agreed to. He wanted a dollar for going over and a dollar for coming back. I paid him on the spot rather than risk the price escalating.

As the old pony pulled the empty cart back to Grand Rapids, Jeff and I pushed off into the wide, fast Saskatchewan River. It brought back memories of battling the Ottawa.

We made an early camp so I could cook bannock. As a treat I added cinnamon to some and raisins to others. Seven bannocks sat on a log to cool while I went to the river to wash my mixing pot and wooden spoon. I was bent over, scrubbing fine gray sand in the bowl, when I looked up to see four Indians in two canoes sweeping around the bend, moving fast, paddling with the current. They steered toward me and pulled their canoes up on the beach beside *Muriel.* They were dressed in buckskins. I figured they were like other Indians we had met, that they talked English when it benefited them, but these Indians spoke only Cree. I made signs inviting them to come to our fire, share a pot of tea.

I brought the four Indians in, and Jeff, who was stretched out in front of the fire dozing, snapped to, sat up cross-legged Indian style, and was very attentive to our guests. It was plain to see they were blue-blooded bush Indians.

I poured tea, the four of them sharing one cup, passing it around. They eyed my bannock and I offered, "Have some bannock," and motioned for them to eat. Eat they did! From across the smoky haze of the fire, I watched these wild men devour one loaf after another, oohing and aahing over the cinnamon and raisins. I read the same untamable quality in them as the deer I stalked on Superior, brown eyes constantly darting, alert to danger, ever ready to fight or flee.

Inwardly it pleased me to think these bush men, who had survived on bannock since infancy, should make such a big deal over my bannock. But at the same time I could sense I was being taken advantage of. I had heard it said there are only two ways you can get into trouble with an Indian, when you try to hurt him or when you try to help him. I began to think these Indians were as corrupted by the white man as their brothers and sisters we had encountered to the south.

"Chis-ta-mow," spoke one of them and withdrew his smoking pipe from a possibles sack he carried at his waist. He tapped it, motioning me to fill it with tobacco and repeated, "Chis-ta-mow." I filled their communal pipe and Jeff and I rolled cigarettes.

When they finally rose to depart, I was so damn disgusted at allowing myself to be a patsy that I didn't bother to walk them to their canoes. They had wolfed down all seven bannock and as everybody knows, bannock translates into miles. They had gorged themselves on our miles. And topped it off with our tobacco. I sat burning with resentment for having allowed it.

Then I saw one of the Indians return carrying a front quarter of a moose. He rolled it off his shoulder and onto our tarp, turned and strolled away like it was nothing. But giving us the meat was a marvelous gesture. It was one of the most stirring and dramatic moments in my life. Here we were, basically greenhorns to the Far North, being paid the highest possible compliment by bush Indians. It was a beautiful feeling to be appreciated. For a second I was misty-eyed, and I noticed Jeff was, too. I recovered and ran down to the riverbank to give a wave of thanks, but when I got there the Indians were gone. Despite the wide gap between us, I felt as though we remained linked as bush brothers.

Jeff and I cooked a feast, stuffed ourselves with moose steak, cornmeal mush, and tea. I told Jeff that if our friends in New York could only see us now—full stomachs, warm fire, somewhere in the wilds of Canada, living with the Indians—they would go nuts.

The meal would have cost a minimum of three bucks at Schraffts, and the steak would not have been moose. That led to a discussion of the memorable restaurants where we had eaten. Later I took out the maps and figured we were still 1,250 miles from Fort Chipewyan. That put a bit of a damper on my high spirits. What if freeze-up occurred early this year?

We continued upstream and portaged into Cross Lake. The sun, dripping streaks of red and yellow over a flaming sky, dropped below the horizon. All the land lay in a quiet hush broken only by the rustling of leaves. The leaves did not have that green punch to them anymore; they were beginning to curl and color and they chattered in a collectively loud voice when the wind blew. In the past few weeks I had been aware of long Vs of geese heading south and sallies of ducks following suit. Most of the birds that sang from the bushes had gone. I paddled and steered, noticing all these changes, and my mind idled drowsily on the bosom of such a glorious evening.

As shadows robbed the colors from the day, we swung ashore and camped. A moon that seemed full of snow ascended from the flat gray of the lake. Summer had slid over the southern horizon. In the morning the grass was cold, there was no mist and no dew. It was a crisp morning, like mornings on the Russian River during prune-picking season.

We portaged from Cross Lake to Cedar Lake and managed five miles before a raw, cold north wind forced us to seek shelter. We set the tent to get out of the wind, and when there appeared to be no letup, I suggested to Jeff we sleep with our clothes on and be ready to shove off at a minute's notice. We could travel by moonlight.

I awoke twice, and the wind was angrily shaking the tent. It blew through the expanse, reverberating around and over and off things. A wind that came from who knew where, rolling up canyons, across flats, carving the landscape, mocking, deceiving, and emphasizing the solitude.

The third time I awoke, the wind had begun to taper. We made a run up the lake only to get trapped in the dark on a mud flat. There seemed to be no solid ground, so we napped in *Muriel* and waited for the sun to return.

When we were again able to travel, we took advantage of a steady crosswind and sailed across Cedar Lake to the narrows, and then returned to battle the current of Saskatchewan River. Cedar Lake and Cross Lake made bulges in the river much like a snake that has swallowed a pair of field mice. We tracked, portaged and paddled upriver to The Pas.

The Pas was full of history. The first white man in the area was Henry Kelsey who came in the 1690s in the service of the Hudson's Bay Company. The first outpost was built by the great French explorer La Verendrye, the discoverer of the Rocky Mountains. We found a quaint settlement of rustic cabins with boardwalks connecting the various business establishments; we spent an hour purchasing everything from tooth powder and grub to underwear and overalls. We really splurged on two fine, red and black plaid wool mackinaws. Let it rain, let it snow! We would be warm.

There was no mail waiting for us at The Pas, so Jeff took out the letters we had received and read them aloud one by one, while I sailed up the lackadaisical Saskatchewan. He arranged the letters by person and date. It was amazing to see how people had changed, the tone of their letters running the gamut from sharing our experiences, with comments about things we had written, to brief pages torn from the scrapbook of their personal existence.

I even let Jeff read Sidney's letters, "poopsies" and all. Sidney. She had not written in several weeks . . . or the letters had not caught up to me. That was a possibility. Who was I kidding? Not myself. Sidney had found someone else and she felt guilty about continuing to write. He better treat her good. She was a lady. If the circumstances had been different, we even might have married. But she was in New York having a gentleman open doors for her and take her to dinner, and I was in the bush killing wild game to eat. The gap between us was not measured as much in miles as in the fact she was content to be normal, and I strove to raise myself above mediocrity. My horizons were unlimited. I was chasing a dream, attempting something no one had been able to attain. I would take my place in history along with the discoverers and early explorers. Really, looking around at the endless landscape uncut by rail or road, reachable only by water, it was apparent the country had changed very little since the days of men like Alexander Mackenzie. What he had seen, we now saw.

We were on schedule—if the weather held. If it was a typical winter, we would have ample time to reach our winter headquarters at Fort Chipewyan. But the threat of an early freeze-up hung like a storm cloud over our heads.

In the following days, we climbed the current of the Saskatchewan River. Along the banks the leaves were turning shades of yellow and red, and the air was crisp. The sun throbbed on and off. Unruly mobs of young clouds gathered in the blue sky and surged full of threat toward us. But generally the weather held.

It was a relentless striving for miles. Miles. I came up with the profound thought that one mile does not a journey make, but each mile added together makes the journey.

Indian summer. Frosty mornings and hot afternoons. I wrote in my log: "The days are getting shorter, colder and windier, and we are doing the best to put the miles behind us, anxious to reach Fort Chipewyan."

We arrived at Cumberland House portage in time to help an Indian transfer poles from a scow to a horse-drawn wagon. In return he allowed us to add *Muriel* and our gear to the load and portaged us three miles to Cumberland House.

The settlement was an unimpressive cluster of Indian tents and shacks. It smelled of rotting fish and too many dogs. The dogs greeted us with howls. While Jeff started dinner, I hiked to the Hudson's Bay post for supplies. The clerk on duty, Jack Ross, was very interested in our expedition. He gave me an exceedingly tender price on my purchases. I felt indebted to him. He insisted on closing the post and taking me to the home of the post manager. How could I refuse? The three of us drank tea and conversed, although I knew Jeff had dinner waiting. When I felt the time was ripe to break away I did, but by then it was dark. I made it to our campfire like a moth drawn to flame. Jeff was already in his sleeping bag, faking sleep, judging by his efforts to snore discreetly. Burned mush pancakes and dry duck sat in the skillet at the edge of the heat. I tried to chew a strip of duck but had to wash it down with water.

In the morning, for only the eighth time, Jeff beat me awake. From the moment I saw him, sitting rigidly on a rock in front of the fire, both hands wrapped around his cup, I knew he was angry. I said, "Good morning," cheerfully. He was mute. I tried to put myself in his place. He was mad, and in part, justifiably so, because he had made a special effort to cook a nice dinner and I messed it up. I was mad because he was still mad. But later, once we were on our way, we were able to talk; I explained I felt obligated to visit since I was given such a good price, that I was performing public relations, that I broke away as soon as I could. I even apologized for being late, although I felt an apology unnecessary. Jeff was being overly sensitive.

We crossed Cumberland Lake and at Sturgeon Landing met an Indian putting traps in a skiff. His plan was to cache them along his trap line now so he would not have to pack them later. He informed us the river we were about to take, the Sturgeon Weir, was considered the "toughest river in the North."

The Sturgeon Weir was shallow and full of rapids. We tracked *Muriel* upriver one mile and made camp. The northern lights shimmered like windblown curtains, sometimes shooting out rays, and I was sure if viewed from space it would look like a halo of fire ringing the pole.

In the morning our progress was as heartbreakingly slow as I feared it would be, and Jeff and I took turns wading in the water, tracking *Muriel* upstream. At the head of the rapids the river flattened; we made a sharp bend, and the prettiest, most peaceful, and colorful river on God's green earth was stretched out before us like a wonderful looking-glass. The sun was skewered on a spiny ridge. The river ran molten and slow, and the surface split for fish feeding on dying insects. A long sigh of wind shimmied the colored leaves, and they hissed at the deep blue of the cloudless sky. A pair of pintails flushed from rushes and startled me. I could feel the delirious cadence of their wing beats drumming my chest. I took a deep breath and shuddered at the beauty of it all.

A beaver swam ahead with a branch in his mouth. I wiggled *Muriel* and motioned for Jeff to stop paddling; then, using the beaver's blind spot, I brought Muriel's bow up until it was impossible for the beaver to ignore us. He forgot his stick and slapped his tail against the water so hard it sounded like the crack of a .30-.30. I back-paddled and waited until I saw him climb out on the bank, following a well-worn trail into the underbrush.

We made forty miles that day. I suppose I should have been content to settle for that but instead I told Jeff one more mile and stretched it into two. Jeff was wise; it was not the first time I had used this little trick. He pouted. I detest pouting. My philosophy is, if something is on your chest say so—don't pack it around.

Of course, I was up first in the morning. I flipped back the tent flap and saw, on the placid water of the little bay where we were camped, a plump mallard drake. I reached for the rifle beside my sleeping bag and took careful aim. I held my breath, squeezed the trigger. The duck fluttered in death. Jeff groaned and rolled over.

I skinned and cleaned the duck and had the meat cooking before I woke Jeff. He was surprised because he had never heard a shot. I thought to myself, "How in hell is it possible to be so unconscious?"

The Sturgeon Weir alternated from an idyllic stream to squalling, snorting rapids foaming about the teeth of mossy rocks. I thought how a river stands for so many things: a life source to fish, reptiles, birds, and animals; the highway of the bush men, their arteries across the continent. A river flows from high point to the ocean, a silver knife flashing and slashing at the earth. It is a patient struggle, one intended to endure for millions of years. Each time the river is convinced of winning, the earth splits or shifts or burps up lava, and the raindrops have to start again, clawing, carving, flattening.

It was raining. It started with no warning, till rivulets of water ran in my eyes. I blinked and rubbed at the ticklish sensation like a child wiping tears. As we came to a portage I was almost glad it was my turn to carry *Muriel;* at least I would escape the rain.

Along the portage we met a trapper transporting a freight canoe and a winter's supply of grub. He made many small trips, ferrying things on his back a couple hundred yards, setting them down, and going back after another load. When we found him he was about all in, so we lent a hand and helped him get to the head of the portage. I pitied his futile, lonely existence and before we paddled off I gave him a magazine I had picked up in Winnipeg, *Mystery Digest*. I had read it many times and had the stories memorized. To me it was excess baggage, but to the trapper it was a fascinating gift that would give him hours of pleasure. He insisted we take the duck he had shot. Later we availed ourselves of a favorable tailwind and sailed Dog Rapids, a stretch of water I knew the trapper would have to portage. I thought of him back there, probably sitting on his cases of foodstuffs reading Mystery Digest. So went life in the bush.

A day and a half later, forty-seven miles and still fighting lingering showers of the storm, we reached Pelican Narrows. The most prominent structure was the red-tiled roof and the white painted siding of the Hudson's Bay post.

Frank Reid, a young Scotsman, managed the post. Via short wave radio he had heard we were coming and graciously insisted we accompany him to his home to meet his wife and share a pot of tea.

Mrs. Reid was a lovely lass with flaming red hair and so pretty it was painful to look directly at her. I wished I had taken a bath. I wished I had cut my hair and shaved. When she handed me a delicate china cup and saucer, I thanked her and concentrated on overcoming my brutish fear of chipping one of them. She passed me a plate with Scottish shortbread and several varieties of cookies and insisted I try one of each.

Mrs. Reid was the perfect hostess and Jack the perfect host. He asked questions and listened attentively to the answers. I sought to learn more from him about the Cree Indians. He educated us in the sad reality of Indian life, saying the Crees were industrious and hard working, but every year a few more left the bush for Winnipeg or Regina or Saskatoon. Once they went away, they never returned. Those remaining continued to stare down the barrel of another culture.

The afternoon fluttered to darkness without my realizing it. We were asked to spend the night and gratefully accepted. Mrs. Reid prepared a thoroughly civilized, home-cooked dinner, and in the afterglow of several glasses of wine, we listened to a radio program originating from Radio City Music Hall in New York. It amused me to think the long arm of radio could reach all the way to Pelican Narrows. Radio signals were everywhere, circling the earth and bombarding space. No place was too remote.

Jeff and I slept on the floor, and in the morning Mrs. Reid made breakfast. Not only was she an extremely pretty woman, she was a consummate cook. As a result of this overwhelming hospitality, we got a late start but fortunately picked up a tailwind that pushed us to Medicine Rapids. We tracked it and returned to sailing.

We played hopscotch from lake to lake with an occasional river tossed in. Every morning the weather was perfect, and in the afternoon the wind would fill our sail and rustle the leaves. The reflection of the brilliant yellows and reds made it look like hot colors were dripping into the deep blue Indian summer sky.

As we portaged from Drinking Lake to Nestowish Lake, a storm was building. Thunderheads boiled, took over the sky and turned so dark they were almost purple. A cold north wind began to buffet us and raindrops as large as pennies splattered the surface of the lake. Thunder boomed. Streaks of lightning ricocheted in the distance, and with the storm moving in our direction, we steered toward shore, ran *Muriel* up on the beach, and huddled helplessly under the sail while the lightning flashed and the thunder crashed over us. Burned ozone hung heavy, and rain clawed with gray fingernails at the land. The runoff bled into gullies.

With the storm retreating we threw back the sail. The blue water of the lake was roiled muddy brown. I felt shell-shocked. Even my equilibrium was upset.

We fought the after-effects of the storm for the remainder of the day. It kept raining; we were soaked to the bone, and the temperature was a good thirty degrees cooler than before the storm. Was this a prelude to an early freeze-up?

Landing at Stanley Mission, we were miserably cold. My teeth chattered, and spasms of shakes left me feeling weak and drowsy. Jeff stepped on shore and his legs buckled. I had the same problem. It seemed to be a short circuit between our brains and muscles, but we managed to shuffle past the mission church to the Hudson's Bay post. The clerk, Jim Law, quickly responded to our dire straits by tossing a few pitchy chunks of wood on the fire. He lent us dry clothes and we drank warm tea to thaw our insides.

I relaxed and felt extremely sleepy, but Jim and a friend of his, Alec Grey, kept me awake. Alec was fluent in Cree and he taught Jeff and me some of the most important words: kim-me-wun (rain), mis-poon (snow), noo-tin (wind), ki-sin-now (cold), oo-ne-kup (portage), up-pe (paddle), and chee-man (canoe). I thought it important to know directions and learned north is kee-wa-tin-nook; south, sow-wa-nook; west, na-ka-pa-hun-nook; and east, wa-pun-nook. Later the four of us went to Jim's cabin and played bridge until midnight, when they finally let us sleep.

I was hoping for an early start in the morning, but Jim insisted we tour the church. I knew I should contemplate the church's 80 year-old existence and its congregation of trappers, Indians, and half-breeds, but I could not. I was anxious to get back on the water. We could not afford to be pissing time away, or freeze-up would catch us short of Fort Chipewyan.

It was difficult extracting ourselves from Stanley Mission and the glowing friendship of Jim and Alec. It was a real temptation to call it quits, as our hosts suggested, and spend a fun winter with them. But if we stopped we would be fighting an uphill battle next year.

At noon we departed with a tailwind and sailed through the narrows of Mountain Lake. At the head of the next portage we met an Indian family, and I tried out my Cree on the man. "Kim-me-un," I made a sweeping gesture at the gray sky. He shot me a grin and emphatically nodded his head. "A-hey," he told me and I took it he concurred. He presented us a small sack of potatoes and, to show my gratitude, I gave him tobacco. We parted company as friends.

It rained. We paddled and portaged. At Great Devil portage, a steep mile climb, I carried the canoe without setting it down once. The day ended on a high note. I threw out a plug and caught a nice pike. The second one hit faster than the first and the third almost jumped over the gunnel for the plug. The fish were in a feeding frenzy.

We ate fish for dinner. Jeff hit the sack but I lingered over tea, smelling the wood smoke and watching the moon glide through holes in the clouds. The night animals sensed this was their last chance of the season. The frogs sang a cheerful goodby before burrowing into the mud. Mice and shrews spoke in shrill squeaks of last minute hunger pangs. A long flight of honkers traversed the night sky. They were pulling out before it was too late.

The following morning we nearly met with disaster. We put *Muriel* in the water too near the rapids of Roah Trout portage and were sucked into the sworl. In my opinion we would have made it to shore if we had continued to paddle, but Jeff jumped overboard and tried to hold onto the tracking rope. The water was too deep—he let go. Instinctively I dropped to my knees and pulled the paddle in a big arc to turn *Muriel* downstream. I picked my way between boulders. It was an exhilarating, slightly frightening experience.

I shot through the rapid and at the foot was spit into a quiet pool. A moment later out popped Jeff, sputtering, thrashing the water. I picked him up, and he held onto *Muriel's* side until he could walk ashore. I built a fire so he could get warm and dry, but it really didn't matter because, within an hour of returning to the water, we were overtaken by a downpour. Eventually the rain subsided, and the sun succeeded in finding a crack between clouds. A glorious rainbow arced across the sky. I mentioned it to Jeff; he looked directly into the sun and asked where the rainbow was. I said a little more sternly than I should have, "When was the last time you saw a rainbow looking into the sun? Dummy!"

On the morning of September 15 I woke up to see fog draped over the trees. Fog held tight to the river, smothering it. Ghost breath.

Jarring me awake was the sight of snow. Only a half inch at most, but it painted the land with an innocence it did not deserve. The green of the pines was iridescent. The yellow leaves were shiny gold. I had been dreading this sight. It meant the surface of the land had cooled enough that snow would stick. The sun rose, played peek-a-boo with the clouds and melted the snow. But that did not erase the fact that snow had stuck.

A back-biting wind chased us around the apron of Churchill Lake. We turned our mackinaw collars up to keep it from breathing down our necks. In the afternoon the clouds thinned, and irregular shadows marched across the landscape as we portaged into Peter Pond Lake.

Peter Pond, for whom the lake was named, fascinated me. He was an early day explorer and one of a handful of Americans involved in the northern fur trade. In researching for our expedition, I had learned he was born in Connecticut, had run away from home at age sixteen, and had gone to sea before he realized his future was as an explorer and fur trader. He spent several years in the Great Lakes region learning the ropes, and then thirteen years in the drainage of the Saskatchewan and Athabasca rivers.

Peter Pond discovered the route leading from Peter Pond Lake, to Lac La Loche, and over the portage to the Clearwater. This was the only section of our travels for which we had no maps. I remembered thinking at the time we would be vulnerable, putting ourselves in the same situation as in *Lure of the Labrador*. I had thought we would worry about it when we got there. Here we were.

We missed the lob stick, the tree, usually a spruce, with all the limbs cut a few feet below the top making it an easily recognizable beacon to mark the foot of a portage trail.

After we realized we missed the portage we came to a blazed tree and thought surely that had to mark an alternate route. At first the trail was cleared and well-marked but soon it deteriorated, and blazes were infrequent. Darkness overtook us; we switched off, one staying with *Muriel* and the other using the candle in a collapsible lantern to search out the next blaze. Finally we were forced to set dry camp. In the morning we hacked our way through the underbrush and came out on a river, a crooked river that was forever doubling back to bite its tail.

The clouds were dark gray and spit snow on us. The water gulped the snowflakes, but on land the snow coated everything with a fine dust. We stopped once and built a fire to warm ourselves, and I shot a duck as insurance. If we were on the right river we should run into Methye Lake and the Hudson's Bay post. If not . . . .

It was a strange feeling that threatened to consume me, hour by hour the feeling getting stronger, that Jeff and I were lost.

We continued, and the gnawing sense of being lost ate at me. This was exactly what had happened to Wallace and Hubbard. One mistake, one wrong river and Hubbard paid for it with his life. A voice inside repeated, "Turn around, retrace your steps to the lob stick and the proper portage."

I gave us one mile and then one mile more deeper into oblivion, or to salvation. Finally, around a sharp bend, crowded close to the river, was a stack of loose hay, a beautiful sight. A symbol of human habitation.

Northwest Territories

Great Slave Lake

CANADA

Fort Smith

Fort Chipewyan

Manitoba

Hudson Bay

The Pas

Grand Rapids

Lake Winnipeg

Ontario

Quebec

SASKATOON

Fort Alexander

Saskatchewan

WINNIPEG

Fort Frances

Thunder Bay

North Bay

MONTREAL

Lake Superior

OTTAWA

Hudson River

Lake Huron

Lake Michigan

NEW YORK

Jeff handling the main sheet, sailing the
French River into Georgian Bay.

The *Seaforth*.

Shell with wolf
pelt.

The narrowest stretch
of water on the route
from New York to Nome.
Bear River, Ontario.

Shell portaging
around rapids.

Shell with muskrat on Winnipeg River.

Right
Shell in camp
baking bannock.

Below
Shell on portage.

Below right
Portage trail in
Saskatchewan.

Jeff with *Muriel*, drying out gear after a wet sail,
Ile a la Crosse

Jeff with Indian on 12-mile portage from
Methy Lake to Clear Water River,
September 22nd, 1936.

Arriving at Fort Fitzgerald.

CHAPTER 15

We followed the river to the Hudson's Bay post. As Jeff and I unthawed by the stove, Mr. Ambrose gathered the supplies on our list. The North has its own brand of etiquette, and foremost is never to ask a direct, personal question. But I could tell Mr. Ambrose was having a difficult time wondering what had driven two wild men to his far-flung outpost. He tiptoed into conversation, asking where we were headed.

"Fort Chipewyan," I told him.

"Chip, ay. Little late in the year for that."

He stumbled onward, wanting to know, "Well, where did you come from?"

"Peter Pond."

"Where before that?" He was curious.

"The Pas."

"Before that?"

"Winnipeg."

He smiled when I said that. "Oh, you started from Winnipeg."

I was beginning to enjoy it. "No, we came over from Superior."

He let out an exasperated sigh. "Well, where in the name of God did you start?"

"New York."

His jaw flopped open. He looked at us with profound respect and said, "Gentlemen, I apologize all over this bloody post. Indeed, you can get to Chip. You can get to China, if that's your destination. New York! You obviously know what you are doing."

While warming ourselves with a cup of tea, I happened to mention our .22 rifle. Mr. Ambrose shook his head in dismay and said we would be better off with a small gauge shotgun that allowed a killing pattern of shot instead of a single slug. He offered to trade a single-shot .410 and two boxes of shells for our .22. It was a charitable gesture on his part; he could never come out on the trade. We did need a shotgun. Without hesitation I agreed to the deal. Mr. Ambrose closed the post, walked us to the water, and saved us the trip to bring back our .22. We paddled away, and he traipsed back to the post.

An Indian village marked the foot of thirteen-mile Methye portage. We hired an Indian and his mare to portage us. The fellow fixed a travois with two long poles and a tarp stretched in between. We loaded "Muriel" and our gear. The horse started with a jerk. She was a sad excuse for a horse. She did fine for a couple miles and then slowed to a snail's pace. At the six-mile mark she gave out entirely.

"She just finish portage. She tired. Give her hour. She be fine," the Indian had the gall to tell us. I knew better and told Jeff we should drop the packs, one of us stay with them while the other accompanied the Indian and his pathetic horse over the portage with *Muriel*. Jeff offered to go, and instantly I looked forward to spending time alone. It would be a beautiful few hours. After they left, I built a fire and stretched out in front of it. The flames cracked and popped. I was so relaxed I fell asleep.

I awoke with a start. Raindrops were hissing in the orange coals. I added wood to the fire, pulled the sail over my head as protection from the rain, and wrote in my log. I was several days behind. Before we had begun our adventure, we had both agreed to keep daily logs, so that the book and movie would be an accurate reflection of the expedition. Jeff had forsaken his log so long ago, I doubted he would ever catch up.

The rain stopped. I shrugged off the sail, stretched, walked up the trail a ways thinking I might catch Jeff and the Indian returning. It was a marvelous feeling being able to roam without the confinement of *Muriel's* slender seventeen feet. But most of all it was inspiring being free of Jeff's stifling presence. There were things about him I simply had to endure: disturbing habits, his snoring, his grogginess in the morning, his moodiness. I'm sure it cut both ways. I must have irritated him; perhaps my pushing got him. I was the engine and he might have resented it.

I reveled in being alone, and the world around me came into sharp focus. The forest charged the air with its pungent smells. The air was crisp, pure and exhilarating. The azure sky shaded to the most delicate tints of blue on the horizon, and fleecy clouds, like handfuls of cotton, flecked the sky. A few small birds flitted and twittered in the brush near me although I could never see them. A dozen crows marched down the sky, cawing, making their southward course known. Downhill from them was a grove of birch, and a swirling wind shimmered the yellow leaves, tugging at them, setting them free to drift like so many bright feathers. One of the last horseflies of the year buzzed me. I allowed him to land on my shoulder; then, with a vengeful slap to make up for all the bites, I killed him, picked him up by a wing and tossed him into the fire.

I wasted time trying to imagine what it would have been like to be a fur brigadier. It was the fur trader who opened the country; his key was the beaver. Three good beaver pelts would bring an Indian a knife, and a five-foot stack of pelts could be traded for a musket. And it all came about because of a haberdashery fad in Europe.

I walked up the trail again. The late afternoon sun sputtered between clouds, and my shadow stretched before me, black and solid. I was anxious for Jeff and the Indian to return because we still had to portage the packs and it was getting late; but at the same time it was damn nice to have Jeff out from underfoot. I did not always mean to knock Jeff. I admired him because he never complained and he worked like a mule. He was every bit as hard-headed as a mule, too. One thing that irritated me was his refusal to learn how to tie a knot—any knot. A bowline was all he needed. His idea of securing *Muriel* was to wrap the painter around a limb or an exposed root a dozen times, and he thought that was supposed to hold her. My aching ass. We went round and round.

I kicked a small rock up the trail and returned to the fire, wishing that Jeff would wake up, start enjoying his surroundings, and learn to tie a decent bowline. Just to keep busy I filed the ax and sharpened my knife. Shadows stretched and darkness crept over the land. I worried. By nature I am not the worrying type, but in this instance I listened to the little voice in me that questioned, could there have been an accident? A cold rain started falling. I tugged at the bill of the yacht cap given me by Mr. Falk, remembering the blonde. But even that was tarnished by a strange sense of foreboding I could not seem to shake. I kept coming back to Jeff lying out there somewhere. What if he stepped in a hole, twisted a knee, and the Indian left him? Maybe at that very moment he was dragging himself over the portage trail. The wind gusted, blowing the cold around and straining through the trees.

At ten o'clock they were still not back. I stoked the fire, so I could be gone up to an hour and still find it, and headed up the trail carrying our candle lantern to illuminate a few feet in front of me.

"Shell," Jeff called my name. "We're coming in. I can see the campfire."

Jeff, the Indian, and his poor old horse straggled into camp. I poured tea and listened to Jeff tell how the horse had quit and how he shouldered *Muriel* and advanced it to the trail head. The Indian said his mare needed a rest, that tomorrow she would pack the gear and not break a sweat.

The three of us slept under the sleeping bags opened like blankets. The Indian was in the middle. He was rank, smelling of a mixture of body odor, horse sweat, fish, and I don't know what else. Rain sputtered again in the middle of the night. I threw a log on the fire and pulled the sail over us.

In the morning the horse, with a great amount of coaxing and tugging on her lead rope, pulled our gear to the head of the portage. Jeff and I shoved off into the broad flow of the Clearwater River, and it was great to be traveling with the current again. How many weeks had it been? And now all that remained was a sixty-four-mile hop to Fort McMurray on the Athabasca River and the 300-mile run to Chip.

September 25, five months to the day from our New York departure, we paddled into Fort McMurray. It was about what one would expect of a frontier settlement: one muddy main street, with cabins strewn across an open flat. Huskies were staked out all around and enveloped the area under an umbrella of noise.

We left *Muriel* on the dock of the Canadian Air Force base and hiked to the post office. There, an envelope from Wiegers with a copy of *Physical Culture*, one of Macfadden's pulpy magazines, awaited. It carried a story about us, a farfetched crock of bull. Whoever had written it had distorted and mutilated fact. We came across sounding like a couple of city kids on a silly escapade, with our sole goal being to recapture health. I was steamed at Wiegers, steamed at Macfadden for publishing it.

I suggested to Jeff we stop by the pub for one beer before returning to the river. We walked in to a celebration. A group of fly boys were celebrating their return from a successful rescue mission of a downed flier. They insisted we join them. I suppose it was our looks, our beards and long hair, that made them nickname Jeff and me Jesus Number One and Jesus Number Two. I was Jesus Number One. We had a hell of a good time, but after an hour, and half a snootful, we returned to *Muriel*.

We found the Athabasca, with the constant tug of its current, the ideal river to paddle and make time. The water now was crystal clear, and yellow and red leaves rolled and tumbled in slow motion beneath the surface, flashing color. Timbered hills crowded close, and it snowed and sleeted and hailed. We stopped several times to build a fire and warm ourselves.

Once we came across a cabin with smoke issuing from a rock fireplace. We stopped and met a trapper named Pete. We drank tea loaded with sugar and he showed us his picture collection. The snapshot that impressed me most was Pete posing, rifle in hand, beside three dead grizzly bears. He told me, "Was four of 'em but I rans outa shells." He entertained us with a couple gigs on his accordion, then we bid adieu and shoved off into a snowstorm looking ahead to the next fire.

Making forty miles a day as we were, it became obvious that Chip was a cinch. The weather was holding. Storms would pass over, dumping snow, but always the sun popped out. Day by day the light became more feeble, and I knew a coat of white that the sun could not erase would eventually lie over the land.

I figured we had two weeks, maybe even three weeks, before freeze-up. I mentioned to Jeff we might want to consider continuing. We would have a straight shot, 300 miles from Lake Athabasca down north to Great Slave Lake, on one of the largest rivers of the interior, Slave River. It would be the last to freeze. We could winter on the Slave River at Fort Fitzgerald, Fort Smith, or if we were lucky, we might even make Fort Resolution on Great Slave Lake.

Jeff was ugly. When I mentioned we should think about going on, he whined, "But we agreed we would winter at Chip before we ever left New York."

"All I'm saying is we ought to consider it," I told him. "It would make it easier next year."

Coming onto the delta at the mouth of the Athabasca, we were discussing whether or not we should go on or stop at Chip. Actually we were arguing. I told him he was short-sighted, narrow-minded, and stubborn not at least to consider getting a jump on next year. He told me I was bull-headed and my thinking asinine.

He wanted a coin flip and I told him, "No. This isn't a democracy." This was too vitally important to be determined by fate. But to soothe things I said, "Let's wait and see if Chip is the kind of place where we would want to winter. If we like it, great. Otherwise we go on to Fitz. From there we'll see."

We found the channel leading into Lake Athabasca covered

for more than a mile by a sheet of thin ice. Rather than take a chance on the sharp edge cutting "Muriel's" skin, Jeff sat with feet over the bow, breaking the ice with his heels. I provided the propulsion; ice tinkled against itself as we slid through. The last six miles we took a chance and made a dash over open water to the cluster of buildings. Fort Chipewyan was a larger settlement than I expected. Upon landing, we went directly to the Hudson's Bay post to check things out. The clerk was busy adding a column of figures. He had a bald spot on the top of his head that he tried to conceal by combing a few strands of hair over, fooling no one, not even himself. When he looked up at us, he peered over wire-rimmed glasses. Then he took the glasses off and carelessly tossed them on the open ledge book. A smug look spread over his face like a warm blush and he drawled, "The hot-shots out of New York. About time."

I took offense with the term hot-shots but said nothing.

"We've been taking bets on when you'd show. Money said we'd have to go get you." He used a collective we. "We figured they'd be fishin' your bodies out long 'fore here."

He produced a yellowed clipping from the *Knickerbocker Press* that he said a friend had sent him. It was a story about Jeff and me with the sentence about our wintering in Chip underlined. The clerk tapped the underlined section, fixed his eyes fatefully on me, and said, "You're ours. You can spend the winter filling us in on the details of your thrilling adventure."

The way he emphasized thrilling and adventure I knew he was mocking us. We had never before had to face this sort of negative reaction, and it took only a split second for me to decide I did not want to spend the winter at Chip. When I spoke, I made sure I was in control and told him evenly, "Sir, my partner and I have made 3,500 miles—through thick and thin, hard times, stormy times, buggy times. We made it, and we will be the ones to decide where we call it quits for the winter. I don't care what it says in the newspaper. We're going on."

I barked a string of supplies we would need, and the clerk knew better than to protest. As I called things off, he would go get them and pile them on the counter. Jeff stood quietly off to one side, resigned to the fact we would be tempting freeze-up.

We scooted around the edge of Lake Athabasca with a cold frosty wind fresh from the Arctic blowing snow on us, our hands freezing to the paddles. I knew just by seeing his rigid outline that Jeff was furious. Our friendship had been distilled to the point of animosity. Let him detest me. But I was right. He would thank me next year. Now he could hate me. What did it matter? What did anything matter? We were only a pimple on the rounded ass of the world.

We turned into the outlet of Lake Athabasca, Rocher River. I killed two ducks, both on the wing, and we ate them that evening, twenty-three miles from Chip and only six miles from the entrance to Slave River.

Slave River was double the size of the Athabasca, with a current so strong the surface in the middle was wavy, a condition created by the faster water over-running the slower, deeper water. As long as we stayed in the current the miles ticked off, but when we steered to shore to make a fire and warm ourselves, Jeff would have to break a fringe of ice with his heels.

We lived without speaking. Jeff operated in his own bubble, a world unto himself. But we worked together as we always had. Working together was rote. You did that without thinking. We had to work together. That was an absolute.

We had as forlorn a camp as there ever was. The bare, cold wetness of a block of ice squatted over the land. I huddled close to the fire while Jeff slept. Out there in the darkness the river gurgled and hissed, and the north wind groaned through the stunted poplar and spruce. Later the wind died, and the quietness became overwhelming. There was absolutely no sound at all except for the river. No frogs. No loons. Life had pulled back from the Far North. The fire popped and sent a shower of sparks into the night. The sparks melted into stars in the heavens. Smoke curled creating images and illusions. Alexander Mackenzie, a small lean man dressed in fringed leather and fur hat, appeared. I had read all the books in the library about him. Fifth Avenue Library. The big doors. The musky smell of leather. Soles scraping marble. People in slow motion. Pages flipping. A sneeze. A cough. A man blowing his nose into a handkerchief. A woman, coat in her lap, reading a German newspaper. Animation. Life.

I became aware of a floating sensation. I could not swear that I had not left my body, traveled to New York, and entered Fifth Avenue Library. The sensory details had been so sharp and powerful. What the hell was I doing? I scared myself. Was I bushed? Bushed as hell.

I needed something concrete, something I could hold on to; I chose my log book. I wrote some in it, turning it to catch the light of the fire on the open pages, and then flipped to the back where I had written a blurb about Mackenzie. He had been right here, in fact he could have camped on this very spot, which would explain the loose spirit running around.

Copied from Mackenzie of Canada was a section about the stretch of water we were coming to, the Rapids of the Damned and Rapids of the Drowned. I read:

When Alexander Mackenzie fought his way through there was neither the Landing nor Fort Smith, nor transport other than the broad backs and toughened muscles of the crew. Some conception may be formed of the dangerous and turbulent nature of these rapids from the fact that in the course of that sixteen miles of rushing water there is a total drop of two hundred forty feet, equivalent to fifteen feet to the mile, but in reality considerably in excess of that at the places where portaging is essential. That stretch of churning, boiling, white water is enough to make the stoutest-hearted voyageurs hesitate before daring to attempt the run. The Indians accompanying Mackenzie lost one of their canoes at the portage called the "Mountain" near which is a dangerous fall. The frail birch-bark craft was in charge of an Indian woman, and in some manner it got caught in the current, was whirled over the falls, and instantly dashed to pieces. The woman managed to escape death by casting herself into the river while there was yet time to save her.

Without a doubt I wanted to see the Rapids of the Damned and Rapids of the Drowned and see the Mountain, too. I wanted to try and take *Muriel* through, to live the experience as fully as Mackenzie had, but the practical side of me weighed the more than equal amount of danger. We could lose our outfit, even drown. It would save time to portage. The scales were tipped.

We made Fort Fitzgerald late the following day, arriving as the paddle wheel ferry "Athabasca" was pulling away from the dock on her last voyage of the season. Jeff and I hiked toward the cabins. At the Hudson's Bay post we learned Fort Fitzgerald and Fort Smith were linked not only by a telephone line, but also by bus service. While we waited for the portage bus, we indulged ourselves at the Portage Hotel in a dinner of roast beef, mashed potatoes and brown gravy, with green beans on the side.

We loaded *Muriel* on top and kept our packs with us as we boarded the bus, the only form of motorized transportation for miles and miles. She ran sixteen miles to Smith and back to Fitz, over and over, and she showed every mile. She was a rusting hulk of scrap metal, held together with wire and twine. We jostled over rocks and crawled through mud holes. Evening drew a curtain over the land, bouncing headlights illuminated a narrow tunnel, and wipers slapped at lazy flakes of snow that fell heavier and heavier as we progressed.

There were about three inches of soft, powdery snow on the ground, and it was still snowing sporadically when we pulled into Smith. I jumped on top and handed *Muriel* to Jeff, who leaned her against the side of the Hudson's Bay post. We got the packs and went inside to see what arrangements we could make for storing "Muriel" and finding us a room for the night. The snow would be over in the morning, and we would go on to Fort Resolution. It should only take a few days more.

The clerk saw us, nodded, said, "They're waitin' fer ya." He motioned outside. "Take the stairs."

I had no notion who "they" were, and it was apparent the clerk was not going to offer. Curiosity led me outside and up a long flight of stairs. The snow squeaked and the stairs groaned under my weight. I could hear Jeff behind me. At the top was a landing, protected by a railing, and a door. Yellow light leaked from a crack under it. Muted tones of men's voices filtered to me as I rapped on the door. Immediately it was swung inward, so fast I felt as if I were being sucked into the room where cigarette smoke hung thick and stale and an oil lamp flickered.

A voice, cut by a heavy British accent, blustered, "Ya bloody canoeists. By God, you're here. Gentlemen, we're glad to see you. But tell me, where the hell have ya been? We been waitin' fer ya."

The man introduced himself as Ken Weaver, said he was a Mountie. He was about my size and build, with rugged good looks that undoubtedly made him popular with women. Instinctively I liked him. He was evidently the leader of the group, for he grabbed an Imperial gallon crock off the table and poured about three fingers into two tin cups, handing one to Jeff and one to me.

"To your health and to a job well done," toasted Weaver and threw back his head and gulped his drink. I immediately did the same. The 180 proof Hudson's Bay rum hit me, searing my esophagus and turning my stomach into a roaring furnace. I lost my wind. I leaned back against the cool wall, managed a partial breath, and blinked away tears stinging my eyes. Weaver was pouring another round. I found my voice harsh as I asked, "How do you drink it like that?"

Weaver shot me a grin, produced another jug and dryly commented, "We always add a little Slave River water." This time he cut the drink.

Besides Weaver, Reg Wells was there (we had met him at McMurray in the pub), Jimmie Boyce, Sid Lago and a couple of radio boys. But it was Weaver who impressed me. He was one two-fisted son-of-a-bitch with an Oxford accent, willing and able to express himself on any subject. We drank, smoked cigarettes, and talked.

Jeff went off in a corner and played cards with the radio boys. Weaver and I and Reg and Sid kept up a running banter. One of the things we discussed was sleep. Weaver contended the position one assumes will determine whether or not a restful night's repose is achieved. He said a man should always lie with the top of his head pointing north. His explanation was that the magnetic earth creates currents flowing from the pole, and that if you face correctly, the currents will flow through your body and out the soles of your feet. As an analogy, he said it was the same as stroking hair: stroke it the way it grows, and it's soothing; stroke it against, and it's irritating. To someone in New York, I'm sure Weaver's theory would seem absurd but to me, at this time, in this place, he was convincing.

I was given tips on the best way to survive the coming months of winter. Reg said not to leave an ax out in the cold overnight because it made the blade brittle. I was told never to wear mukluks on the same foot two days in succession—that they would last twice as long if switched every day. Never gather the night's wood near water because the moisture would cause it to shoot off live coals and sparks that might damage an outfit. And half a dozen other well-meaning pearls.

It turned out to be a terrific, extraordinary evening. One by one the others passed out. And then it was Weaver and me. Weaver told me, "We're going to have a beautiful winter."

"Oh no," I protested, "we're going to Resolution." I was feeling drunk and slurring my words.

"You're not going to Resolution. The lads there are all piss-heads. There's a lot more doin' here."

I wanted to object but was too tired. My eyelids felt as though they were shades being pulled down.

"Besides, tomorrow you're comin' with me to look for the body of an Indian," commented Weaver. The last I remember, he was pouring himself another drink.

PART TWO

CHAPTER 16

It must have been three or four hours later. Weaver was shaking me awake, his words booming and crashing like cymbals in the hands of a madman. A groan escaped me. I struggled to rise, only to discover we were stacked like cordwood.

Weaver stuck a fresh crock of rum under my nose; my instinctive reaction was to gag, but instead I disengaged myself from the pile up, and to show that rootin' tootin' Weaver what I was made of, I took half a swig of rum, held it, cut it with another half swig of water, swished it around and gulped. For a moment I feared I would be sick, but I overcame it.

Weaver and I were on our fourth drink of the day when the others started stirring. Weaver admonished them for "sleeping the day away." The last to open his eyes was Jeff and then only after Weaver threatened to pour a drink into him if he did not.

"I need volunteers," announced Weaver. He pointed to Jeff and me. "You and you."

Hazily I recalled something being said the previous night about hunting for the body of an Indian. I had not agreed to anything. I started to protest, but Weaver brought me up short, snarling, "By God, you're goin'."

I guess I had had just enough rum to dampen my motivation for getting to Resolution. A compelling voice told me to stop, that it would take only a few days to get to Resolution in the spring. It looked like Smith had the obvious potential as a great wintering spot. Resolution would be a pig in the poke. There would be no Weaver at Resolution. He was one of a kind, a blood-and-guts sort, but educated, too, a dichotomy.

Weaver grabbed the crock, roared, "Let's get a move on," to Jeff and me and headed out the door. We were left to rummage through our packs, taking the essentials for a few days in the bush, primarily sleeping bags and a change of clothes. After arranging with the clerk at the post to store *Muriel*, we hurried to catch up with Weaver at the RCMP dock.

There was a half-foot of powder snow and our breath was visible as we hurried on our way. An engine cranked over, caught with a roar. Weaver goosed the throttle a time or two as we came into view. Three Indians were already seated in the back. Jeff climbed in and crawled under the bulkhead. I pushed us off and took the seat beside Weaver. Before we got underway, Weaver and I had to have a drink. He backed out and kicked the inboard in the pants. We flew downstream. Wind swept back my hair and made tears run out of the corners of my eyes. I cupped my hands and hollered, "This is the only way to travel."

Weaver shouted back, "Bloody right."

An eagle turning tight circles above a riffle in the water saw us coming and climbed. Every so often Weaver would hand over the rum and I would drink, cutting it with a cupped handful of spray from over the side.

After about an hour Weaver throttled back and turned the boat up a small stream. He moved cautiously, scanning the water ahead for obstructions and steering around them. Here, where the reduced engine noise made conversation possible, he informed me of the details of our mission. Francois, the Indian sitting in the middle, had accidentally shot and killed his uncle. They had been moose hunting.

"We'll find the body, look at the evidence, see if it matches Francois's story, and bring the body back," explained Weaver. I glanced at Francois, who had the longest face and the saddest eyes I ever hope to see. I was along for the ride. Helping my buddy Weaver. Having a little excitement. The river closed off on us, and we beached on a sandbar. Within minutes we had a fire going. Weaver and I and Jeff stood around it while the Indians went hunting. We drank and Weaver recited poetry, his version of Robert Service's "The Shooting of Dan McGrew." The land was hushed and Weaver's voice melodic:

> "Were you ever out in the Great Alone, when the
> moon was awful clear,
> And the icy mountains hemmed you in with a silence
> you most could hear;
> With only the howl of a timber wolf, and you
> camped there in the cold,

A half-dead thing in a stark, dead world, clean
mad for the muck called gold;

The music almost died away ... then it burst like
a pent-up flood;
And it seemed to say, 'Repay, repay,' and my eyes
were blind with blood.
The thought came back of an ancient wrong, and
it stung like a frozen lash,
And the lust awoke to kill, to kill ... then
the music stopped with a crash,
And the stranger turned, and his eyes they
burned in a most peculiar way;
In a buckskin shirt that was glazed with dirt
he sat, and I saw him sway;
Then 'Boys,' say he, 'you don't know me, and
none of you care a damn;
But I want to state, and my words are straight,
and I'll bet my poke they're true,
That one of you is a hound of hell...and that
one is Dan McGrew...."

Weaver had the perfect voice, rough like rocks banging against
each other, and his delivery was faultless. He recited "The Cre-
mation of Sam McGee," and I got a ticklish sensation along my
spine, at the base of my neck. And while the poetry flowed, four
well-spaced shots were discernible. The Indians returned with
four ducks for our lunch.

After we picked the bones clean, we all shouldered packs; the
Indians broke trail, and Weaver and I and Jeff worked on the
crock as we traveled. We finished it at night camp. The Indians
rolled up in blankets, and Jeff crawled into his sleeping bag, but
Weaver and I went on and on trading stories and jokes and what
have you. He could not best me and I could not best him, and we
had a hell of a time trying.

"Up and at 'em. Get a move on, you lazy pokes," Weaver
berated us. It seemed I had barely closed my eyes. I drank coffee
and watched Weaver fix breakfast and lunch—bacon bannock.
After that we shouldered our packs and started off across a plain
dotted with scrubby willow brush.

The day was steel gray, the sky and horizon welded together.
We stopped at half past noon, built a fire, drank tea, and ate
bannock. While we were there, an Indian came into camp; he had

come overland from Smith leading five horses. One of the horses was pulling a travois loaded with an old-style Indian birch bark canoe.

When it came to choosing our individual modes of transportation, Weaver said he would take the canoe, and I was figuring to go with him, but Jeff claimed he was inexperienced with horses and would feel more comfortable in the canoe.

"You don't mind riding with the Indians, do you?" asked Weaver.

"Hell, no," I told him. In the short time I had been around the Indians I had concluded there was much I could learn from watching them. Perhaps I could learn more of their language. The horse I was given was slow but steady. We rode in a loose band in almost complete silence. The country duplicated itself time after time with bare flats and willow patches. I wondered how the Indians could tell where we were, how we would ever meet up with Weaver and Jeff.

Late in the afternoon I smelled faint traces of smoke and then spotted a thin column on the far side of a thicket. It was about that time Weaver whistled. When we got to camp Jeff was sleeping, using his sleeping bag for a pillow, and Weaver was relaxing with his bare feet exposed to the warmth of the fire. He sipped his tea and in a very serious tone remarked, "Jesus, Taylor, I thought you and your friends were lost." I laughed. What a remarkable sense of humor he had.

The following day we were up early looking for the body of the Indian. According to Francois, this was the area where the accident had occurred. By afternoon we became discouraged and left the Indians to conduct the search while we returned to the fire. Weaver had kept up on the Olympics and filled us in. The United States had won all the sprints, hurdles, and the jumping events. He suggested we hold our own bush Olympics. We decided on a sprint—to a jack pine about seventy-five yards out and back to the fire—a standing broad jump, and a running broad jump. Weaver won all three events. I placed a close second in everything but could not quite match Weaver's athletic prowess. Most impressive was his eighteen-foot mark in the running broad jump, especially considering the loose footing and hard landing.

The Indians had no luck finding Francois's uncle. In the morning Weaver sat Francois down and told him to retell the details of the killing. It was very difficult for Francois. He stared hard into the fire for the longest time, either trying to remember or getting up the courage to speak. His English was not good. He mixed Indian words in his story, and his voice was as soft as a breeze through a grove of quaking aspen. He told about the fateful morning, the moose grunting in the brush, the sound of his rubbing antlers on a tree, quick movement, the shot, and finding his uncle. He started crying, no sobs, just tears rolling over and cascading off his brown cheeks.

Weaver told him, "Happens. You wish you could have that moment back, but ya can't. You'll always have a black hole in your soul. I believe you. I'm not going to arrest you. Take me to the body."

Francois led the way across frozen swamps and willow patches, the country covered by a sugar coating of snow. He went straight to the camp he previously had been unable, more likely unwilling, to find. There was a tent, undisturbed, and a coffee pot sitting atop black ashes. A hundred yards out, in the willows, we located the body of Francois's uncle. Outwardly, from all the signs, it appeared Francois had told the truth. The dead man was slumped over a small windfall, shot high in the back, a pipe on the ground by one hand. He must have been bent over knocking out ashes, probably coughing like smokers do. Francois heard what he thought was a moose grunting and rubbing his antlers, saw a dark form partially obscured by willows, and fired.

The body was frozen and perfectly preserved except for the side of his face lying on the ground; it was a dark bluish-purple. The way he was, he would not fit on a horse's back, so Weaver and I took turns working his legs back and forth enough to allow tying him over a saddle western style.

We took the body to Salt River where the RCMP boat was moored and on to Smith.

CHAPTER 17

Fort Smith was a cluster of white government buildings, a few frame houses, and many log cabins and Indian shacks. Smoke that rose from rock fireplaces and stovepipes formed a dirty cloud above the settlement. The population numbered about 200 souls, with Indians far and away the majority. There were four or five times more dogs than people and they kept up a continuous chorus of howling.

We got back from recovering the Indian's body and made the rounds with Weaver, drinking a crock of rum and visiting his friends. We had dinner at the Club Cafe and afterward Weaver made arrangements for Jeff and me to take over a government cabin that was not being used. But we never saw it that day. We ended up back in the room above the Hudson's Bay post drinking with the boys.

Our cabin was nestled in the trees at the edge of the police compound. It was white with green trim, board and batten over logs. It was the nuts, one room and not particularly spacious, but adequate. No one had lived there in several years. We gave it a good cleaning and settled in.

Weaver had given me the past six months of *Esquire* and the book *Appointment in Samarra*. I liked John O'Hara. He never wrote anything bad. Jeff spent his time BS-ing with the radio boys. At night we would get together, Weaver, me, Sid, Reg, Jeff, and his radio buddies. Sometimes we met at the Club Cafe and other times at the room above the post. One night it was suggested we needed a club house, a place where we could congregate. Sid, bless his big-hearted soul, offered his porch if we would help him clean it. We threw ourselves into the task. Sid had spent his life hunting and trapping and trading. We removed snowshoes, dog harness, fish nets, rifles . . . and found enough furniture to have two tables and eight chairs. There was even a pane of glass Sid didn't know he had that fit the window. "Sid's" was open for business. He served sandwiches and coffee at a nominal charge. The conversation and good times were free.

Each Canadian citizen was entitled to a permit, one Imperial gallon of liquor, customer's choice, each month. Friends might not know one another's birthdays, but they most certainly knew the day permits were scheduled to come in on the mail plane. It was custom that a permit be shared. A permit was an excuse for a party. And Sid's became the place to party and drink, not a private club, but open to anyone and everyone, including our Indian friends.

One evening Weaver and Sid and Reg and I were working on a permit of rum when four Cree girls, all giggles and flirting glances, came in and sat at the other table. Three of the girls were overweight and not anything special but the fourth was young and cute—sort of cute. I winked at her, and from the twittering at the table you would have thought I had tickled her on the most sensitive part of her body. Weaver, seeing what happened, laughed.

Using a phony British accent to mock Weaver, I said to him, "Say, ol' chap. If you wanted to crawl in the sack with an Indian girl, how would you go about it?"

Weaver ended his hearty laugh and told me, suddenly serious, "Pick out the one you want. Go over and ask her if she knows where your cabin is. Tell her you'll meet her there."

"Come on." I was misbelieving.

"Give it a try," he challenged.

I took a swallow of rum, and with perhaps a bit of an Errol Flynn swagger, I took the necessary few steps to the other table and said to the cute one, "My name's Shell Taylor." Apprehension tugged—what if I had been set up as the butt of some monstrous joke? But I charged ahead. "Do you know where my cabin is?" She nodded yes. "Meet me there."

I returned to our table as triumphant as Caesar returning from the second battle of Philippi. When I looked back, the girl was slipping out the door. I waited ten minutes, that was all I could wait, and followed her. As I approached the cabin in the white moonlight, I saw smoke belch from the chimney. Someone had opened the damper. Beautiful.

CHAPTER 18

The wind surged, carrying with it the cold of the Arctic. The land and even Slave River froze. The sun was an insignificant fuzzy ball riding the hip of the southern horizon. It packed no punch whatsoever.

Jeff and I spent our time cutting wood and lazing around, reading, playing bridge, drinking permit liquor, and occasionally arranging dates with Indian girls. We lived together but actually we spent very little time together. Jeff liked to sleep in. I liked to get a jump on the day. Most mornings I would hike over to Sid's and what happened that day depended on who would wander in.

One afternoon Jeff and I were both in the cabin. I was baking bannock and noticed out the window a squat figure coming toward our cabin. It was evident we had a visitor, someone I did not recognize.

The stranger introduced himself as Mike Dempsey, chief buffalo warden of the Arctic Wood Buffalo Park. He asked Jeff and me to accompany him on a buffalo hunt.

"Have you fellows ever mushed dogs?" Mike wanted to know.

"Every morning to the office in New York," I replied. He got a good chuckle out of that and withdrew a jug from the folds of his parka and set it on the table. We drank and talked about the upcoming hunt.

According to Mike, the wood buffalo was the largest mammal in North America, mature bulls weighing 3,000 pounds and standing seven feet at the withers. They were related to the extinct European buffalo and had been driven to the edge of extinction by meat hunters in the early 1900s. In 1915 the government passed a law making it a crime to kill a wood buffalo. Every year since then, the native herd had increased in size, until finally the animals had to be thinned.

"The only natural enemy of a wood buffalo is the wolf. A wolf will kill anything," said Mike, and then warned us, "You shoot a buffalo, make it a kill shot. If you don't, they take it unkindly and charge. Hell of a dangerous situation. If one does take after you, save your ammunition—don't try a head shot. The bullet will ricochet. Wait until the bugger drops his head and let him have it where the shoulders and neck come together. The bullet will tear up his heart." Mike promised to furnish Army issue .303 Ross rifles, dog teams, toboggans, government rations, and the honorary title of "Deputy Rangers."

The next morning, true to his word, Mike sent around a couple of his underlings with dogs for us. Jeff and I spent the next few hours learning the intricacies involved in handling and driving a team of dogs. We were advised never to leave the toboggan flat on its track at the end of a day's march or it would freeze to the spot, and always to tend to our dogs before tending our personal needs. We were shown how to break up fights between dogs, grabbing them by the scruffs of the necks and pulling them apart, how to harness the dogs, and then, the various commands necessary to drive, turn, and stop a team.

The first lap I took around the compound—riding behind those burly government dogs, frozen flecks of ice stinging my face—was an experience I will never forget. Adjectives like invigorating and stimulating are weak and dead. We literally flew, dogs lunging at the weight of the toboggan, and me on back trying to keep my balance.

One time I passed the radio building, and one of the boys stepped out and called that Hearst was reporting Roosevelt had won re-election. To me, on the back of a heaving toboggan, trying to control a team of charging huskies, the outcome of the presidential election seemed totally irrelevant and inconsequential.

The morning we departed for the buffalo hunt, Weaver swung over to wish me luck. As a result I was late leaving, and my dogs were whining with impatience. I yelled at them to mush, or "marsh" as the French-Canadians taught us to say, and the dogs tore away with such an instant burst of speed I was nearly left behind.

Besides Mike, Jeff and me there were two rangers, Lawrence and Collins, and two Cree Indians on the hunt. It was prearranged that others would meet us, to bring supplies and take out meat.

Our dog teams traveled single file. I was last. We crossed a broad plain interlaced with low rolling hills, skirted stands of spruce and jack pines, thickets of naked willow, birch, and poplar.

The country was composed of interlocking creeks and small streams that at other times of the year would be swampy, slimy green pools of brackish water laced with sphagnum islands covered by moss, a breeding ground for mosquitoes. But now the impenetrable bog was sealed and we glided across it, mile after mile.

I watched my dogs and admired the way they worked together. Tom, my lead dog, was raw-boned, hard-muscled, predominately white with a black face and brown eyebrow markings. One of his ears drooped from a long forgotten fight, and he wore it as a badge. The other dogs, May, Jerry, Bissto, Roy, and Wop, were lined up one after another, Canadian bush style, and I memorized their markings and any traits I could identify about them, measuring them to see how they worked. I was paying attention to the superficial things instead of seeing the first subtle warning that one of my dogs was in trouble. It was May, a bitch and the lightest and oldest dog. She put everything into matching the other dogs, and when she ran out of gas, she dropped. I took her out of her harness and laid her in the toboggan. Within a few minutes she revived; however, the remainder of the day she was content in the toboggan. I felt sick about running her in the ground, but Mike told me later that such things were common until the dogs were in condition.

Our base camp was Mission Cabin on a tributary of Salt Creek. We chained the dogs to cut-off willows and fed them a mixture of corn meal and tallow heated in a big black kettle over a fire. The dogs wolfed it down with tails wagging.

I, too, had a big appetite. After filling my belly I settled back, enjoying the warmth of the cabin and the cheery glow of a fire. One of the Indians started playing a harmonica. I have never been a fan of the mouth organ but that evening, amidst the rustic but comfortable surroundings, anticipating the upcoming hunt, I savored the moment and the sense of camaraderie we shared.

During the night I was awakened by the feral howling of our huskies, and mixed in was the calling of a pack of wolves. I could imagine the wolves, sneaking through the timber, keeping in the moon shadows, trying to coax the huskies into joining them. If one ever did, it would be killed. I lay awake for a long time, listening to the drama, but eventually I drifted off into contented sleep.

Next morning after breakfast we divided into hunting groups. I went with Collins and the Indian Isodore. The first day we failed to get within range of a bull but the others did well, bagging three. Jeff killed a big one.

The second day Collins, Isodore and I hunted again. Within a mile of Mission Cabin, we spotted four buffalo about a thousand yards out headed toward a timbered island. Isodore stayed with the dogs while Collins and I made a broad circle, keeping the timbered island between us and the buffalo. We worked ourselves into position and the buffalo cooperated. The ambush was set. We lay on our stomachs in the snow as the buffalo appeared, walking from the timbered island into the open.

"All bulls," whispered Collins. My heart was hammering, partly from exertion and cold—the temperature was below zero—but mostly from the thrill, the prospect of shooting my first wood buffalo. I raised the rifle. I had never fired the gun but Mike was familiar with it; he had told me it shot a foot low at a hundred yards. I took several deep breaths to steady myself, expelling the air out of one side of my mouth so the vapor would not impair my vision.

"Take the lead bull. Wait. On three. One. Two. Three."

We fired simultaneously. The butt walloped my shoulder but I kept my eye on the target and saw a quick geyser of steam vent into the cold air. My bull went down but was right back up, trotting. I jerked back the bolt, ejected the spent casing, and slammed a fresh load into the chamber. I shot again, and again, and again, each fresh wound venting steam as the first had, until my bull finally went down for keeps. Collins fired five or six times at his animal, I lost count.

The two remaining bulls ran in confused circles before lining out and heading for the timber on the far side of the plain. I swung on the closest and sent him crashing on his shoulder. He regained his feet and charged into the willows.

I had been taught never to allow a wounded animal to suffer. I started after my second bull. Collins called, "Wait!" I ignored him and went on.

If I had had any experience as a buffalo hunter, I would have taken the time to roll and smoke a cigarette, allowing the bull to lie down, stiffen or die. Instead, I charged right in, and when I got to where he had gone down, there was a bright splash of crimson in the snow. I had hit him in a vital spot.

The trail led into the willows. I looked over my shoulder and could see Isodore bringing the dogs across the plain and Collins already involved in the process of gutting one of the bulls.

The bloody trail was a boulevard that weaved through clumps of willows. I shuffled along in a ready crouch.

I glanced down to step over a windfall and when I looked up, he was there, forty feet away, black beady eyes staring, nostrils alternately flaring and closing, blowing steam and blood. His head went down. He charged, eyes rolled back showing only white, head canted to one side snowplow fashion, blood pouring from his nose and mouth. I waited. Waited as Mike had directed. He was almost to me. I shoved the muzzle forward and jerked the trigger. Kerwam! A fraction of a second later he hit me in the right buttocks with his God-awful head. I realized I was scrambling on all fours, without my rifle, seemingly in slow motion. It was like a dream where you are moving as fast as you can, but it is still so agonizingly slow. That helpless feeling. He was somewhere behind me. I reached a small spruce, maybe five inches in diameter, and climbed it quick like a red squirrel being chased by a marten. I was clinging to the top of the tree, swaying slightly, six or eight feet off the ground when the shakes hit me. It was an uncontrollable reaction having to do with fear. I suppose it was the adrenaline in my system. When I finally overcame it, I shinnied down, retrieved my rifle, and found the bull a hundred yards from where he had hit me, leaned up against a tree, dead.

From my point of view, that was by far the most exciting incident occurring during the hunt at Salt Creek. In all we took thirty bulls. The meat was transported to Smith and from there distributed to various Indian missions.

There was to be a second buffalo hunt in the Hay Camp area, sixteen bulls to be taken, and Mike invited Jeff and me to keep hunting. We returned to Smith first, tended the dogs, fed them, and then heated water and took turns enjoying a bath in the big wash basin we used. After that we caught up with the party at Sid's.

The next morning we were away early with the lot of us suffering hangovers. We traveled south, the frozen Slave River our highway. Under the silver skin was the Rapids of the Doomed and Rapids of the Drowned. We mushed past Fort Fitzgerald to Buffalo Landing and veered cross-country to Hay Camp. There was a log cabin there. The interior was one large, open room, with bunks lining the wall; the tin stove and chimney oven were the focal point.

During the night a chinook wind commenced, and the temperature rose fifty degrees. Most of the snow melted. We could not hunt the next day, so we killed time playing penny ante poker, chewing the fat, and reading. Weaver had lent me his copy of *The Shape of Things to Come*, and I was taking my time with it, enjoying the story instead of rushing through to the conclusion. I knew people in New York who read the last page first, and if that looked interesting, they might then read the whole thing.

The chinook petered out, and the temperature skidded to more normal temperatures. It snowed. The hunt was on again. We hunted hard, but the buffalo were scattered, and after a week we had only three bulls. Mike told me we would be out at least another week and would likely run low on tobacco. He asked if I wanted to make the thirty-two-mile run into Fort Fitzgerald and I told him, "You bet." I needed to get off on my own.

In the morning the thermometer on the side of the cabin registered 44 degrees below zero as I harnessed the dogs by lantern light. Mike came around and informed me, "On your way you'll meet Jack Streeter. Streeter has a permit. He will try to pass without sharing a drink. Don't let him. But a bit of advice: in the cold it gets to a man fast."

I thought about Mike's warning and concluded alcohol interfered with thinking and out on the trail a single mistake could prove to be a fatal one.

The silver sparkle of the stars anticipated the emergence of the sun and began to dim. I pointed my dogs toward Fitz and headed down the trail. My dogs wanted to stay with the others who howled long and sad at our departure. I kept them going.

We outran the noise and the air took on a stimulating stillness, where my own breathing and the snow squeaking under the toboggan were the dominant noises. The sky was hard, luminous as stainless steel. Now and then the cold would cause a jack pine to explode with a sharp crack. I reached Slave River, and the two-foot-thick ice began to split in long, lightning-shaped cracks with the appropriate roll of thunder. The north country groaned under the weight of the cold.

I spotted my first large herd of migrating caribou, thirty-four crossing ahead of us on the ice; the dogs caught the smell and went crazy, running in an all-out sprint. I hung onto the lazyback and rode. When we reached where the caribou had crossed, the dogs wanted to follow. We had a serious disagreement but it was reconciled, and we proceeded toward Fitz.

Every eight or nine miles I stopped, built a fire to warm myself and brewed a pot of tea. The closer I got, the more the trail deteriorated. I had to get off sometimes and help push the toboggan through the drifted snow.

I had a feeling of remoteness, that my dogs and I were an exceedingly small speck, and I looked forward to meeting Jack Streeter. I wanted to have the drink to warm me from the inside out. I fantasized. But the closer I came to Fitz, the more certain I became I would not meet Streeter. Just when my disillusionment was strongest, my lead dog Tom whined and picked up the pace, and I knew there was another musher on the trail. Streeter saw me coming and stopped, but our pleasantries were interrupted by the dogs. As usual they wanted to fight, so Streeter drove his team a few feet past before they settled down. He wanted to know how the trail was and I told him.

"How's the buffalo hunt?" he inquired.

"Not good, they're scattered."

"Cold enough fer ya?"

"Yep."

The small talk continued without Streeter's letting on he had a permit in his possession. He never offered me a drink. Finally I came right out and said, "Jack, didn't you pick up your permit today?"

He was sheepish. "How did you know?"

"Everyone from Fitz to Aklavik knows."

"Want a drink?"

"Thought you'd never ask." I smiled. He dug the jug out of his bedroll and I took a drink, allowing it to warm in my mouth before swallowing it. And since Streeter had not offered a drink initially, I had a second. Streeter reclaimed his bottle and went on his way.

I should have paid more warning to Mike's advice, because the alcohol in my exhausted state out there in the cold really got me. I felt loose as a goose, and it was all I could do to hang on over the wavy, rutted trail.

Ahead was Fitz. I could see the thin blue pencil marks of smoke pointing at the chimneys of the cabins.

CHAPTER 19

We arrived at Fort Smith from our buffalo hunt on December 16, and I headed into the Christmas season with a package from Mother and Dad which included the best seller *Hula Moon*. A book was the perfect present. I read, drank with the boys at Sid's, and worked on a story about the buffalo hunt for Wiegers.

One day Jeff returned from the post office with news. Adam Kemp, who went by the nickname Cappy, had asked him to spend the next few months trapping with him. We had met Cappy on the hunt at Hay Camp, and he and Jeff had hit it off buddy-buddy.

"Fantastic," I told Jeff, "Go."

It made perfect sense. Why did he even have to think about it? What an experience, and furthermore, it would provide a little distance between us. Our friendship, from such steady company, had become an overwhelming pain in the ass. I'm sure the sword cut both ways. Joining Cappy would be for the best all around.

The morning Jeff pulled out, I was up early fixing him a big send-off breakfast. It was sixty miles to Cappy's cabin. After he was gone, I relished the feeling that Jeff was miles away. He would no longer be popping in.

Although it was a little out of my character, I felt apprehensive about Jeff out there on the trail alone. The following day I called to Fitz and was told Jeff had already passed through. That put my mind at ease.

On Christmas Eve I went to Sid's and listened to the Bing Crosby program on the radio. Midnight mass brought together everyone from Smith and the outlying areas. Weaver and I, after indulging in permit rum all evening, decided at the last minute to attend mass.

The congregation was made up of a half-dozen government men in uniform, trappers with fresh haircuts, and Indian families dressed in beaded outfits. The mix of humanity left no doubt that we were at the outer edge of civilization. When New Year's rolled around, Weaver and I did it up right. We had a rip-roaring time drinking permit Scotch, then went to the dance where music was provided by a squeeze box and a fiddle. The stove in the middle of the room was shimmering heat, and the dancers, Indians mostly, had thrown off their parkas and were swinging each other in circles. The room smelled of wood smoke and body odor. I ducked outside for fresh air.

It had stopped snowing and stars were splashed across the sky like the view of electric lights I remembered from Muriel's Parc Vendome apartment. I wondered how she was welcoming in the New Year and pictured her at the kind of glamorous party she had once taken me. I had met comedian Jack Benny and his wife Mary Livingston; Walter O'Keefe, the host of the Camel Caravan radio program; singer Helen Morgan; movie star Ethyl Barrymore; and all the best band leaders in the world. I remember one party where Tommy Riggs (of Betty Lou fame) went in the bedroom and proceeded to go into one of the funniest routines I ever heard. Betty Lou was his creation, his voice, and she was this wonderful sweet girl on his radio program. But that night when Tommy told her she should go to bed, the Betty Lou voice said, sweet as honey, "Ahhh, Daddy, do I have to? It's not even midnight."

"Get in bed, darling."

"Go to hell, Daddy," said the nice sweet voice and we all gathered around the door and listened to America's darling berate her father with every four-letter insult known to man. It was hilarious.

I was still smiling about the memories as I stepped out in the cold to relieve myself. The parties. Women wearing dresses with a hundred cool corners. Exotic smells. Teasing. Happy, animated people.

I stood there for a moment enjoying the night. It was a few minutes before midnight. Someone got a jump on the New Year and cranked off a round on the far side of the settlement. Other rifles and shotguns answered in bursts like a string of firecrackers, and then it was over. From inside the hall came the muted strains of a fiddle and an accordion, and the hard stomping of stocking feet on a wooden floor. Yellow light strained its way through the blanket tacked over the window. Away to the north, colors were swaying across the sky. The distant moon bathed all in a cold, white light. The snow was blue, and ice crystals shimmered.

When I was through drinking in the night, I took a step, stubbed my foot, and started to fall. Around me erupted a team of sleeping huskies covered by snow. Stumbling into a dog team was one of the most dangerous situations in the Far North. Every winter several people were killed by dogs. A neighbor of ours on Russian River once told me how coyotes will pester a cow about ready to calve. They will eat the calf out of her as it is born and will eat the cow from the tail forward. It might take days for her to die.

I could not stop myself from going down, but I did manage to get my arms and legs under me, so when I hit, I sprang and performed a tumbler's roll to get beyond the range of the snarling dogs.

CHAPTER 20

One afternoon I was at Sid's when Bert Edge came looking for me. "Would you like to go with me on my trap line? I could use your help and I'd sure as hell enjoy your company."

I was flattered that this man of the bush, one of the most respected trappers and dog mushers in the North, would ask me to join him. I told him, sure.

"I'll get you a team," he promised.

I had been spoiled by the big, well-fed team of government dogs that were put at my disposal during the buffalo hunt. When Bert came with my team, I could not help but think they were the most decrepit string of small, timid, underfed dogs ever to be assembled and called a team.

Bert said, "They're Indian dogs but we'll fatten them up and they'll be good ones." I had my doubts.

The morning before we pulled out, I checked the mail and had a letter from Jeff. It was a relatively short letter telling about his experiences trapping and saying he was looking forward to spring, break-up and resuming our travels. I wrote a quick note back.

By midmorning we were on the trail. The temperature was thirty-four below. Bert and his seasoned dogs boiled into the lead, while my mistreated and underfed dogs lagged. They had learned to run on fear, under threat of another beating. They kept turning their heads to see if I was reaching for the whipping chain. I started talking to them, verbally caressing them, as well as stopping occasionally to pet them. But it was not that simple. They would have to learn to respect, trust, and love me before they could ever be a good team.

I caught up with Bert at noon camp. He had caribou ribs

130

propped up with sticks near the fire so they would thaw. I fed my dogs and scratched behind their ears and loved and romanced the hell out of them. When we got started again, they were a little more spirited, but they still kept looking around. I told them, "Okay, you knuckle-heads. I've fed and petted you. Pull."

I lost contact with Bert but was connected to him by the trail he was breaking. The insignificant sun tumbled from the sky and the afterglow was the dull yellow of a gold nugget. A virgin white moon crept over the rim of the flat plain and the northern lights flooded the sky with an awesome beauty; electric currents snapped and sizzled.

The dogs, either sensing or smelling we were nearing the cabin, tugged hard at the traces. I could see a rectangular patch of light and a man's silhouette. I was cold and hungry and anxious to get there, but at the same time I hated for this glorious evening to be over.

Bert helped tend my dogs, and then I accompanied him to the cabin. I stepped through the door and was assaulted by caustic smells. Every bone from every meal Bert had ever eaten there was discarded on the dirt floor. He had skinned animals, and the rancid aroma of mink, beaver, weasel, cat, and wolf was over-powering. It was as if the essence of the north had been distilled. I sluffed off my parka, and Bert ladled stew into a bowl for me. I quit smelling and started eating

That night I slept soundly and never awoke when Bert fixed a pot of tea and departed. I awoke at nine in a panic, not able to breathe, gagging on the stench. I jumped off my bunk and went to work cleaning; I shoveled out the bigger things, swept the dirt and dead flies and animal droppings with a spruce bow, and threw it all behind the cabin. I kicked open the door and let the cold air rush in to replace the lingering smells.

Bert returned and never said boo. I hadn't expected him to. He lived like he did because during the trapping season he became a wild animal. He would not have caught much, smelling of soap. I spent the first couple of days helping Bert lay his trap lines. From the cabin at Trout Lake, we made sets radiating like spokes from the hub of a wheel, snowshoeing out in seven and one-half mile legs. Fifteen miles was about all a man on snowshoes could cover in a day. Caribou were migrating through the country, and we killed as many as we needed, which was considerable as it was the main source of food for ourselves and the twelve dogs.

When we went around to check on the first leg, at a set on a wooded island that was thrust above the frozen surface of Trout Lake, we discovered we had caught a wolf. His comrades ran around in circles, nipping at him, and coaxing him to follow. But he could not.

As we approached, the others ran away leaving the rangy black wolf with his foot in our trap. I was awed by the size of him. He went every bit of 120 pounds. The tip of his fur was tinged with silver and it rippled as he raised hackles and turned on us.

There were all those times around campfires, as far back as Superior, that wolves had talked to me, and I had sensed the urge within me to call out my loneliness to them. Wolves were the heart of my inner spirit. I was like a wolf in ways. I liked the deserted haunts, the solitude, the role of an outcast. I stood thinking private thoughts while Bert waded in and dealt a fatal blow with his killing club across the wolf's nose. It was quick and merciful. The wolf fell over, twitching, muscles convulsing, and then he was still.

Our schedule worked so that we got around to each trap every fourth day, taking what we caught back to the cabin where we had to wait for it to thaw before we could do the skinning. My previous experience, as a teenager trapping along Russian River for coon, bobcat, and skunk, made the skinning of marten and mink easy. The procedure was to use a skinning knife and brute strength to peel the skin off an animal. The head was last and you took great care around the ears and around the eyes because every little nick detracted from the hide and the subsequent value of it. The skin was pulled onto a splint and stretched. Animal hides decorated our walls drying, giving off pungent odors.

Bert was a great teacher. I could live three lifetimes and never gain the knowledge he was born with.

We set No. 2 Newhouse traps for fox. Bert said any larger trap would catch too high on the leg, breaking the bone, and in the cold, the leg would be twisted off in a matter of minutes. Ever after, the three-legged fox would be too cunning to be trapped. We used a No. 3 trap on otter. The spots we selected for trapping were usually on a small creek connecting two lakes, where there were signs of otter. Beaver were trapped below the ice, in a process that involved locating the rounded humps of their lodges and setting traps baited with poplar in their runways. Any time you worked under water, you had to have a fire nearby. It was cold and tiring work.

Our routine repeated: cleaning, rebaiting, and freshening the sets. We killed caribou, wasting nothing, using the entrails to bait our wolf traps. We cut wood. And in the evening when the work was done, we would sit around the cabin playing cribbage and listening to the wolves howl.

When I was a kid, Dad hired an old Swede one summer to help me in the apple orchard. He was a good worker but a sour-smelling old coot. Now after about six weeks on the trap line, I was smelling just like him. I tried heating water on the stove and sponging off, but then I would pull on my same pair of stinking, rotted long johns. I started dreaming about baths, easing into a big tub and luxuriating in the hot water. Sometimes it would be a bubble bath.

Finally it got to the point where I could no longer stand myself, and I told Bert I wanted to make a run into Smith for a change of clothes and a bath. He shot me a quizzical look, said it was fine with him, and that I could take in a load of caribou meat.

My dogs had been well fed and were packing muscles on their frames from bringing in the caribou we killed. One thing about these dogs—and it happened every morning starting out—they would run a couple of hundred yards, then stop as if on cue. One dog would hop over the traces and relieve himself off to the side of the trail. After finishing his business, he would jump into place and away you went until the next dog wanted to do his duty. They had been taught this; otherwise crap would get on the bottom of the toboggan and it would be hard to slide. The process would take anywhere from a half-hour to three-quarters of an hour to get out of the way. I would watch closely, but I could never tell which dog would be next; there was no detectable sign of communication between dogs.

A team has a certain pace, a pace they are comfortable maintaining. When they are fresh, they are up on their toes, loving to run, pulling the toboggan, "Ta-da-da, ta-da-da, ta-da-da." The second day they start to slow, and by the tenth day, they're down to a walk. Then you get the chain--link chain a couple feet long--and you go down the line, starting with your lead and working back to the wheel, beating dogs. One by one, you grab them by their collars and beat the hell out of them. It scares them more than it hurts them. You beat the whole damned team, and it takes a great deal of effort. When you are done, you put away the chain, grab hold of the lazyback, and tell them, "Okay boys—mush!" And away they go, up on their toes, "Ta-da-da, ta-da-da, ta-da-da," running, tails in the air. Ten days later you beat them again.

It was a fact of life in this part of the country--the dogs were used to being beaten. They must have figured if you were willing to invest that much time and energy, you must really love them.

But some of the dogs were horribly mistreated. It would break your heart to see what I've seen. Some owners would go fishing, and the dogs might get the heads and entrails if they were lucky. If a caribou were killed, they might get a few scraps. In the summertime, I'd seen dogs staked out with fish heads in front of them; they were not able to eat because the insects were bothering them so much that their muzzles were infected and bleeding. Some people did think of their dogs and kept them staked on points of land where the natural flow of wind would keep down the insects. But others would chain their dogs to any convenient thing and not even bother to have fresh water available. It's no wonder the poor dogs turned out as they did.

I harnessed my dogs, and we started off with 600 pounds of caribou on the toboggan. I traveled at night because it was colder and the snow was better. As we flew along the trail, the fresh moon was making the snow sparkle and stars were strewn across the heaven like diamonds tossed on black velvet. The bush country was magnificent, so vast, spectacular, and gorgeous.

I reminisced. This was March. Two years before, though somewhat later on—Easter Sunday, to be specific—my Uncle Stan had been in New York, and we had had ourselves quite a celebration. Uncle Stan was on the wagon at the time, so we stuck with something mild, sherry flips. We started at Number One Fifth Avenue Hotel, went on to the Brevoort, up Fifth Avenue and over to the Waldorf, then to the Park Lane, the St. Regis, and finally the Plaza—with stops in between. Walking along Fifth Avenue, we were arm in arm singing, "In your Easter bonnet, with all the frills upon it, you'll be the grandest lady in the Easter parade . . . ."

I found myself singing, and my voice was rolling across the barren, snowy landscape. I thought no one was within thirty miles of me until I popped onto the apron of an open flat and, to my undying embarrassment, there was a musher coming directly toward me. Talk about feeling like an idiot. He must have been listening to me for miles, wondering who the crazy bastard was who didn't have enough sense to keep his mouth shut on such a wonderful night.

The other musher was an Indian and, to make the situation even worse, our teams got into a first-class dog fight. It was pure bedlam, dogs snarling, snapping, growling, biting, rolling around, and getting all mixed. The Indian and I waded in swinging chains and attempting to pull dogs apart. What a tangled mess! Harness between their legs, over their ears, and in their mouths. It took us the best part of an hour to get the fight under control and separate the dogs. After that we parted company.

I continued on toward Smith. A few miles from the settlement I had to go over the drop-off to Slave River. From there it would be a straight shot over the icy highway to the settlement. Bert had instructed me on how to take the drop-off from the prairie. It was several hundred feet down at a forty or fifty degree angle. When I got there, I wrapped the chain around the toboggan to act as a brake, positioned myself to dig in my heels, and started over the edge. I had to keep the toboggan upright and hold it back so it would not overrun the dogs. It was hairy, but what a thrill!

Coming in to Fort Smith, the dogs were prancing, tails up; all the dogs in the settlement howled a greeting. I swung by Bert's cabin, carried the caribou meat up the ladder, and put it where it was safe from animals, on the roof. I had awakened his wife Joan. She put on a pot of tea and when I finished, I sat with her and drank hot, strong tea. She poured us a second cup, and I realized she was acting strangely nervous, not like Joan. I asked if anything was wrong. She bit her lower lip and told me, yes, there was. A man in the settlement was bothering her, wanting her to have sex with him. I asked what she wanted me to do, even offered to talk to the fellow.

"No," she said, touching the back of my hand with her fingertips. "But tell Bert. Tell him to come in as soon as he can, before something bad happens."

After that I went home, heated water, and took a bath, enjoying it, even though I knew I'd have to turn around and go right back out. I pulled on a pair of brand new long johns and a set of fresh clothes, threw the old ones away, and went for a big breakfast at the Club Cafe before going over to Sid's to catch up on the latest happenings. Then it was back to the bush.

The dogs hated to leave. They whined and tried to double back. I showed them the chain. The last beating was fresh in their minds and they lined out.

On the way to Trout Lake I rehearsed what I would tell Bert. I didn't want to make it sound like the situation at home was more serious than it was. I didn't want him to go off half-cocked and kill the other guy. But still, I didn't want to make light of the situation either; Joan was very concerned about her safety.

When I reached the cabin I said to Bert, "This is probably no big deal, nothing has happened yet, but—there is this fellow annoying Joan." He took the news quietly, took another sip of tea, and finally acknowledged what I had told him, saying he would head in, and that I could run the trap line. He would be back in a week.

135

Those seven days were the most pleasurable and satisfying of the winter. I was without a care in the world, alone to trap and traipse around in the bush. And during that week, winter took a long sigh, slacked off, sputtered, and grudgingly gave way to spring. The temperature for the first time in months warmed above freezing during the day, and the sun, riding an ever-widening arc in the sky, actually felt warm. The ice around rocks began to pull back. Icicles that had clung to the cabin eaves all winter let loose their hold and crashed to the ground. Chattering squirrels ran up and down trees. Migratory birds returned, ducks and geese passed overhead, and the melody of birds sprang from the willows. Ice melted, cracked, thundered as it shifted.

Mission cabin and toboggans.

Wood buffalo

Jeff with wood
buffalo he killed.

Two of the Indians
on the buffalo
hunt. Buffalo kill
in the background.

Hauling meat back to Fort Smith after a buffalo hunt.

Burt Edge at Trout Lake cabin.

Shell with dog team.

Shell's wheel dog, "Tuk."

Beaver traps ready to
place under water.

Stretching beaver,
Trout Lake cabin.

CHAPTER 21

The date was April 25, l937, and I was sitting on an exposed boulder overlooking Slave River, contemplating the ice and the water moving below, running deep, dark, swift and clear. It had been one year since Jeff and I departed New York, and I was beginning to see signs that winter would release its iron grip and let us get on with the expedition. Around Smith there were puddles of standing water, and grass was poking through the snow in places. As the snow receded, it exposed garbage. The wind was blowing from town toward me, and I would occasionally catch a whiff of something rotten.

I reflected on those things that had happened in one short year and tried to glimpse the future, imagining what adventures awaited us between here and Nome. While I sat I spotted the first robin of spring; I also got bitten by the first mosquito, which I killed and cursed because it was the start of what would become an onslaught of insects.

Jeff and I had spent the month of April together, waiting for the ice to rot and the break-up to occur. After spending nearly three months apart, we had both been anxious to resume our friendship. When we got together, we shook hands, which at the time seemed awkward as hell. Jeff's disposition and attitude, having been on his own and with Cappy, was much improved. The new Jeff was more positive about things, and more independent. There were a couple times, when he didn't know I was around, that I caught him whistling. I never remembered hearing him whistle before. He was almost fun to be with, and we did things together. We retrieved *Muriel* from the Hudson's Bay warehouse, washed her, sanded her ribs and thwarts and varnished the wood. I painted the canvas with gray canoe enamel, while Jeff cut a stencil and repainted the name *Muriel* in white. Joan Edge sewed the sail for us with seven-ounce duck canvas ordered from Fitz, and Jeff and I hiked into the bush and chopped down a spar.

Several times a day I would find myself checking the river. I wanted to get going and could feel the anxiety rising inside me like spring runoff filling a dam. I needed to keep myself occupied, and so I cleaned the cabin, scrubbing from ceiling to floor, and even painting the cupboard shelves.

The last day of April we received word from Fitz that the ice had moved for a half-hour before jamming and backing up. I waited for any sign of break-up, impatiently pacing from the river to the cabin, and finally hiked up to Sid's where I visited and helped Sid and a friend drink a permit.

The next two days I spent reading *River* by Thomas Wolfe. And then there was nothing to do but to keep checking the river and to be bored. On May 8, the ice went out at Fitz. Two days later, break-up reached Smith. I told Jeff we would pull out in the morning.

"You'll bloody well die trying!" Weaver barked at me when I informed him. "Don't be a fool. Haven't you heard of ice jams? Wait a couple days for the ice to clear." But he could tell I was not to be dissuaded. And the next day he was there on the riverbank, along with most of the settlement's population, to wish us well and send us on our way. I felt a wave of sentiment, not so much because we were leaving friends, but for the sheer personal ecstasy of being back on the water. I took my seat in the stern and felt *Muriel* wiggle beneath me. She was a familiar girl friend, and we had been too long separated.

Jeff pushed off. We waved goodby with the paddles. I looked back once. Our friends were headed up the bank to their homes and everyday lives. For an instant I felt a pang in my solar plexus, brought about, I'm sure, by the realization we would never see them again. But it went away, and my attention returned to the roily water, the chunks of floating ice, and the sweet pull of the current.

"Four more months," I told myself. If we had not reached Nome by then, the fall winds would blow us off the Bering Sea. Suddenly four months seemed like such a short time. I told myself the expedition would end but a man's true journey has no end. Still, this would be the focal point of our lives. Something we would be talking about in old age. We would be the ones who discovered the Northwest Passage. The Slave River was running a tremendous volume, and the swirling surface was obstructed with small chunks and great sheets of floating ice. We paddled a zigzag course, trying to outmaneuver the ice but found it almost as fast to run the bow up on a floating iceberg and hitch a free ride at the rate of about six miles per hour.

The second day we let icebergs carry us to an all-time distance record, making sixty-one miles. We could have added another ten, but several times we had to pull out because of ice jams. The ice would pile up, damming the river, until with a roar, the river would break through. After the surge was over, we would put back in.

We were following the route of Alexander Mackenzie and would be in his shadow until we turned away to follow Rat River over the Rocky Mountains. His party, which included five voyageurs and their Indian wives, embarked from Fort Chipewyan in the spring of 1789. They had two birchbark canoes, one of which was fitted, like *Muriel,* with a mast and sail. It took Mackenzie and his party four days from the Portage des Noyes to Great Slave Lake. Jeff and I made the run to Fort Resolution in two and a half.

The original inhabitants of Fort Resolution were two Northwesters, Cuthbert Grant and Laurent Le Roux, who built a trading post at the mouth of Slave River in 1786. We found the settlement to be a mirror image of Fort Smith, except that it faced out over the bleakness of Great Slave Lake.

The lake was immense, ten thousand square miles. Its shores were indented with numerous bays, some of them deep, which would prolong our travel. But the real problem we faced was that the lake was still frozen. Our path appeared blocked.

We were met in Resolution by a delegation of radio corpsmen; friends in Smith had passed word we were coming. We received a warm welcome, and a party was thrown in our honor. Before I joined it, I took a hike along the edge of the lake and discovered the ice was not a solid sheet but fractured; great chunks of ice had shifted, leaving leads of open water. I perceived we might be able to string the leads together, portaging from one to the next, around the lake to where it discharged into Mackenzie River, 110 miles as the crow flies. It was worth a try. We could not afford to sit around in Resolution, waiting for the damned ice to melt, not if we wanted to make Nome.

I joined the party. It was going full swing with an instrumental playing on the radio and a general hubbub of talk and laughter. One of the radio boys announced to me, "You'll be here a month anyway."

It hit me wrong. I reacted. "Bullshit. For your information, ice melts from shore out. It fractures and leaves open leads. We can follow the open water, follow the leads."

"Never make it," the same fellow retorted smugly. "The wind blows and piles up ice on shore. You can't get around it."

"We'll wait for the wind to blow the other way. Simple," I told him.

"You'll starve waiting."

"We best get started. Jeff." I moved to the door and Jeff reluctantly followed. They had convinced him there was no way we could get around the lake. As we slid *Muriel* into an open lead, Jeff expressed his opinion. "I think we ought to wait."

I informed him, "We're going. That's all there is to it."

Jeff said nothing more. He pushed us off, and luckily we were able to follow leads, portaging from one to the next. But then we reached mile sixteen and were greeted by an impenetrable wall of crumpled ice, forty feet high, pushed up and left by the wind.

We had no choice but to camp. I prayed that night for a south wind, and miraculously the prayers were answered. Sometime before daylight the wind shook the tent fiercely, and later ice groaned and growled; it sounded like the earth being ripped apart. Light revealed something as awesome as Moses parting the Red Sea: The ice had pulled back. There was open water. We scrambled to take advantage of it.

That afternoon the wind reversed itself and forced us to shore. We were stuck there. To keep busy we built an elaborate lean-to over the tent with driftwood. It helped break the wind.

On the fifth day I knew something had to be done and hiked eight miles to a high point. I climbed a spruce, sat up there in the branches like an eagle, and studied the lake. There was one possible route. If we portaged about four miles, there was an open lead that tied in with other leads that would get us several more miles. It was the only way. I started back for camp. The yellow glow of the sun reflected off the ice. The lean-to was silhouetted. The flickering fire was the only sign of movement in all this empty, remote land.

For two weeks we fought our way around the south shore of Great Slave Lake, battling the ice, and constantly portaging. The few times the wind slackened, we were met by clouds of mosquitoes and their devilish torment. It seemed remarkable that the sun had only begun to melt the snow and ice, and already the bugs were hatching.

Once during this trying period, the distant whine of an airplane engine came rolling across the desolate expanse. Jeff and I were in the middle of a portage. We stopped, searched the sky as the sound grew louder and were soon able to make out a speck on the horizon. It appeared the pilot was following the shore line, flying at a low altitude. When it was almost to us, I recognized the plane as belonging to Art Rankin, a flyboy from Smith. He spotted us and circled, dipping his wings. Jeff and I waved. Jeff was so happy to see someone, and his actions so exuberant and animated, I finally had to tell him to knock it off, or Art would think we were in trouble. Art circled a couple more times and headed off in the direction of Aklavic. Long after he had disappeared, his engine could be heard reverberating across the ice. It faded into the nothingness.

PART THREE

CHAPTER 22

At Point Desmarais we noticed the first effects of the Mackenzie River, a conspicuous pulling that swept us, as well as numerous chunks of ice, into a westward flow. At first, the broad stream, which was about a mile across, was filled with islands and great blocks of ice. I caught myself thinking about Mackenzie and how he must have had such high hopes at that point for reaching the Pacific. He was the first white man to venture into the river's steady current.

We reached the Indian settlement of Fort Providence; as the first travelers of the year, we were big news. We replenished our stores at the Hudson's Bay post and quickly returned to the water.

To the west, the Rocky Mountains, snowcapped and shrouded in a wispy veil of fog, came into view, looming larger with each advancing mile. As we neared the foothills, the river made a sharp turn to the right and began flowing due north. Mackenzie must have known at that point that he could never reach the Pacific, but he went on. In his journal he described this section of the river: ". . . the current has been so strong that it produced a hissing sound like a kettle of water in a moderate state of boiling."

In the swift water, the surface spun tight whirlpools and chunks of ice rammed into one another. We ran these stretches with *Muriel* pulled up on an ice flow.

Back at Fort Providence the clerk had warned us the section of the river known as the Ramparts was a bottleneck where ice jams were frequent and very dangerous. He had told a story about a derelict canoe caught in an ice jam that was lifted and deposited on the top of the cliff. It stayed there for years as a testimonial to the terrible power of the river, but eventually it rotted away.

The river pinched from being a mile wide to less than 500 yards. The depth at this point was said to be 300 feet, and it gave me a bit of an uneasy feeling, wondering what *Muriel* might look like to the monsters of the deep. The canyon we passed through was bounded by rocky limestone ramparts rising 250 feet above the level of the river.

We shot the gap without the ice jamming. After about seven miles, the river spread to a mile and a half wide, and a strong northwest wind challenged us. We could not make headway, so we tried a trick we had heard about. We cut a full-limbed spruce and tied it to our painter; thus we were carried along at the speed of the current, which was running at about five miles an hour.

Jeff and I took turns sleeping. We had plenty of bannock, and being on the water was preferable to fighting the bugs on shore.

I was holding vigil when the head wind faltered and changed to a cross wind. I cut us loose from the spruce, hoisted the sail, and in not quite two hours we made twenty-four miles. That gave us a new record for a twenty-four-hour period of ninety-three miles.

The days were like a spinning top, no beginning, no end, only the constant spinning. The few times we went ashore, to bake bannock or have a pot of tea, we were tipsy, unsteady from the constant motion of being on the water.

After forty straight hours of travel, we arrived at Fort Simpson, a Hudson's Bay post and Indian settlement. It was 3 A.M., we needed supplies, and not wanting to waste valuable travel time, I rapped on the door of the post until the clerk, who had his residence upstairs, awoke and opened for us. Even with the stop at Fort Simpson we topped our all-time best, making ninety-five miles.

The country we passed through was changing from the muskeg that had dominated our travel since Winnipeg to the mountains where snow-fed streams came squalling and snorting, mingling their water with the mighty Mackenzie and becoming lost in it.

We equalled our record of 95 miles and bettered it two days running, with 98 and then 108. It was during the twenty-four hour period in which we made 108 miles that the hallucinations began. The first time they occurred, I was steering and making notes in my journal. The date was June 6, my parents' anniversary, and I was thinking Dad would take Mom to dinner. I looked up from the paper, and to my shock, it appeared we were being drawn into a boiling rapid. I blinked it away. In reality the river was flat as glass. I was unnerved by it. When Jeff awoke I traded places with him; I tried to sleep but could not. Several times I opened my eyes and could have sworn we were going uphill. It was the damnedest sensation.

We passed through a second rampart and this time I saw weird shapes and faces of friends and acquaintances etched in the lime-stone. Mercifully, sleep finally came. I dreamed, dreamed there was a braided golden rope encircling the earth and all I had to do was grab hold and it would take me anywhere I wanted to go. I jumped and jumped but could never reach it. I awoke feeling agitated and still dead tired. It seemed every part of my body ached. I shifted positions and must have groaned because Jeff asked if I was all right; I said I was and left it at that.

"I'm glad you're awake," said Jeff, "I've been seeing some of the strangest damned things. Things that aren't really there."

"Like rapids? Like running uphill? Things like that?" I asked.

"Then you've seen them too," he said, and I nodded.

The queerest phenomenon was that we began to hallucinate the very same things: water off to the side running over a non-existent ledge, sandbars and islands that were not actually there. The images were sharp and precise. Water roared over a ledge sending up a mist, and the sun played rainbows. Trees on islands swayed in the wind. Geese walked on sandbars and cocked their heads to stare at us. Driftwood moved at frightening speeds. Small chunks of ice built into huge ice jams. The snowy peaks of the Rockies emerged from the water, appearing magnified and dis-torted.

"Hail, Muriel!"

I had been napping, but I jerked wide awake and looked to-ward shore. Standing there was a man waving his arms, and be-hind him was the friendly sight of a log cabin with smoke issuing from the chimney.

The man introduced himself as Dominic Fisher. His soiled denim pants needed patching, and his wool shirt was worn to bare thread at the elbows. He invited us to join him for a "spot of tea," and we quickly accepted. We walked into the cabin, and Dominic introduced us to his Indian wife. While we sipped tea, their three children, sitting on the dirt floor, picked over the bones of boiled beaver feet.

Forty miles below Fisher's cabin we came to another cabin, and it was beginning to seem as though we might be on the outskirts of civilization. The old man who lived there, Clark, fixed us moose steak and filled us with stories. He had come north during the gold rush of '98. He told of men striking it rich and men who died trying.

"Come over the hump from the Yukon," he told us, and I asked if he had come by way of Rat River. He shook his gray tousled head, smiled wickedly, drawled, "Yep. She a bastard. If you're going that way it's a 1,400-foot climb in forty miles. Bald-faced mountains. Wind howls. Deerflies big as your thumb, and mosquitoes draw blood a pint at a time." About the time we were leaving, Clark said he wished he were going with us, that he wanted to get back on the Pacific side but supposed he would die right where he was.

We had photographs of the Rat River, given us by the flyboys from Smith; the country appeared brown and desolate, and the river a squiggly white line of uninterrupted rapids. The Rat was going to be our toughest challenge.

CHAPTER 23

Alexander Mackenzie was the first white man to reach the great river of the north and follow it to its mouth on the Arctic Ocean. He lingered for a time hoping to make contact with Eskimos. But with winter coming, he turned his back on the Arctic and made his way toward Fort Chipewyan, the closest settlement, 1,500 miles away.

We followed Mackenzie's route to Point Separation, the entrance to the delta. Here we turned west and picked our way through an array of low islands covered with moss and brightly blooming flowers. During a stop for tea, I investigated and discovered the ground was frozen solid a scant four inches below the surface.

We turned up Peel River and went a few miles upstream before locating Rat River. The much feared Rat River! The Rat would take us to the uppermost reaches of the Continental Divide. We would cross over the hump and be on the Pacific side. This would be our supreme test; all the water we had faced previously was only practice.

The canyon carved by the Rat was a deep-cut V running into the looming Richardson Mountains, the northernmost extension of the Rocky mountain chain. We would have forty miles of the most harrowing rapids to track to reach the summit of McDougall Pass. The water was high and discolored, carrying the muted browns and reds of the mountains.

We started up the Rat, but our progress was slowed by the swift current and the way the river kept twisting back on itself. We would track to the bends, and then if we were on the outside, we would have to paddle across the current because sweepers, where the water had undercut the bank and toppled trees, made staying on the outside too dangerous. If we should wash against a sweeper, the power of the downstream flow would crush *Muriel's* hull. Every step of the way we were dogged by a ghastly black cloud of mosquitoes and deerflies. After four miles of enduring them, and bone-tired from fighting the Rat, we made camp and put up the tent.

The following morning we were back at it. We would trade off—one riding in *Muriel* and pushing with a tracking pole, the other wading through the water pulling the tracking line. The stints in the water were pure agony. It was so cold that about a half-hour was all we could take before our feet and legs began to swell and our muscles cramp.

Each mile we climbed, the river would snarl and growl more loudly and each successive rapid would be wilder than the last. One mistake here, one slip, and our outfit would be lost to the fury of the terrible river.

The canyon of the Rat was like an open wound, devoid of vegetation, the walls steep and scarred. We had entered one of the most remote corners of the continent. Virgin territory. According to old man Clark, only eight outfits had passed this way since the end of the gold rush era. This was as wild as it ever got. There was no trace of man. In the mornings we found signs that grizzly bears had visited the camp. Occasionally we would spot Dall sheep or mountain goats high on a rocky face.

Nothing we could have done would have prepared us for the Rat, especially since it came on the heels of traveling 900 miles down the Mackenzie in ten days. The price we had paid for that was sheer exhaustion that crept into the very marrow of our bones. The hallucinations had been caused by this, plus a combination of other factors, including the atmospheric condition of twenty-four-hour a day sunshine and its reflection off the water. What we had seen was no different than mirages on a desert.

That was a lie. The hallucinations were more real. Thank God we left them behind on the Mackenzie. Once on the Rat, with a regular schedule of sleep, we were not bothered by quirks of the mind.

As we climbed higher, we hit a series of benches where the river would flatten from a hundred yards to a quarter of a mile. Here we paddled. The interludes revealed the extremes the Rat was willing to go to in order to break a man's spirit.

The photographs we had of the Rat, taken at 10,000 feet, showed the precise lay of the land. There was a portage over a ridge that would allow us to reach the summit of the pass much quicker than following the river around. After a steep climb we reached the top and could look down on a breathtakingly beautiful blue lake. I felt like whooping or something, but I was just too damned beat. We trudged on to the lake.

In camp that night Jeff and I talked about the significance of our accomplishment. We had crossed the backbone of the continent. We were the first to have crossed from the Atlantic to the Pacific drainage. I knew we still had some rough miles ahead of us. It was not going to be a cakewalk. We had to find our way to the Yukon, run it to the ocean, and then we still would have 365 miles of ocean travel to contend with. I'm not the kind to rake in the pot until all the hands are shown. At this point I was not going to break an arm patting myself on the back.

After partaking of a dinner of duck and fresh bannock, I felt revived. I brimmed with satisfaction at reaching the point we had. The wild country had been bridged. Soon we would be passing from Canada into the Alaskan territory. Back in the U.S.A. Tremendous!

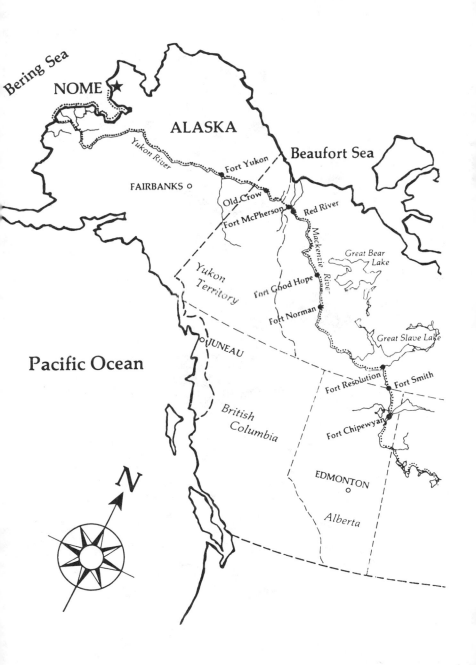

Shell shaving and sailing on the Mackenzie River.

Jeff sailing
on the Bering
Sea.

Muriel on the
beach at Nome,
August 11, 1937.

Shell, *left*, and Jeff, *right*, landing in New York after
expedition.

CHAPTER 24

We ran the Little Bell to the Bell River—a fine stream, fifty yards wide and moving fast—and then into the Porcupine River which was bigger yet. I knew it was silly of me, but I was a little glum. Hell, I was melancholy. *Muriel* would never again track a rapid. After we got back, the Smithsonian would probably ask for her, put her on display. To millions she would be "The canoe used on the voyage of discovery, proving the existence of a water-way across the North American continent. Sheldon Taylor and Jeffrey Pope, 1936-1937."

To me she was much more. She was a friend; I knew her intimately. The cracked ribs that happened when I slipped and fell. I remembered doing it, could see it happening in my mind as if it were a newsreel of a terrible tragedy. But I could not for the life of me recall the name of the portage. I could ask Jeff. It was not that important. And the patches, all the patches. I remembered them individually. A rock we hit. An unseen sharp stick. A jagged piece of ice . . . .

Muriel, she was a companion, a pal, a buddy, a mate. She was reliable. She was special. I chuckled. It amused me that I had a closer friendship with an inanimate object than I did with Jeff. He was too pensive, brooding, introverted.

Three hours of paddling and being swept along in the current of the Porcupine River brought us to a log cabin which sat on a bench overlooking the river. We hiked up and found a caribou hide tacked on the wall and words scrawled with the point of an ashy stick. "Gon Ft. Yukon—Mak sef at ome—B bak son."

I decided we might as well avail ourselves of the trapper's hospitality, even in his absence. We moved in. I started to cook over his stove, and when I looked around, it surprised me to find a two-pound tin of Hills Brothers coffee and a Sears Roebuck

151

catalog. I pointed out the fact to Jeff, but he was not particularly interested.

Jeff won the coin toss to see who had the honor of sleeping in the bunk. It was apparently such a comfortable bed that he was reluctant to get up the next morning. Four times I told him to get a move on. When we finally did get on the water, I mentioned something to him about sleeping in, and he snapped at me, "Shut up." Then he mumbled something. I think he called me a son-of-a-bitch, but I blocked him out, ignored His Royal Moodiness, and concentrated on my surroundings. The country was undergoing a transformation from the bleakness of the summit to the woods, green, dense, and abundant with wildlife. I saw a cow moose and a bull caribou. There were honkers and ducks, teal, buffelhead, wood ducks and mallards. We caught fish, grayling and white fish, anytime we chose to toss out a spoon. We lived well.

The Porcupine carried us to the last settlement in Canada, Old Crow. We arrived to the howling of dogs and a half-dozen Indian children who formed a welcoming committee. They stared. Jeff stayed with *Muriel* so the kids would not be tempted to steal something, and I hiked to the store. It was hard to believe, but we were beyond the influence of the Hudson's Bay Company. Instead of the familiar white building with the red tile roof, I bought supplies, that would carry us the 300 miles to Fort Yukon, at a trading post.

Below Old Crow the Porcupine ran faster, and we guided *Muriel* through rapid after rapid as we dropped into a canyon known as the Ramparts. We made it to Rampart House, a deserted cabin, which marked the border. Just for the hell of it, I sang the national anthem. As usual, Jeff had no response.

The next day, as we slid past a limestone bluff, I spotted a strange bone sticking out of the bank. I swung over for a look-see and discovered it was a large petrified tooth of some prehistoric mammal. For several hours afterward, I tried to imagine this country a million years before, dinosaurs, woolly mammoths . . . .

On the lower stretch of the Porcupine, where the current fractured into many channels and disappeared, a cold west wind blew in our faces and made the going difficult. With rain pelting us and the wind gusting, we had no choice but to make camp in the willows.

By morning the worst of the storm had passed, and we returned to the water, bucking waves, each paddle stroke bringing us that much closer to the Yukon River.

CHAPTER 25

At the confluence with Yukon River, a muddy, sluggish piece of water a mile wide, we turned upstream four miles to Fort Yukon. There was a trading post, cafe, a cluster of log cabins, shacks, and a few tents or Indian tepees. Everything radiated from the dock. It was a large dock and it linked Fort Yukon to the outside world. Two thousand miles of the Yukon, all the way to Whitehorse, were linked by ferry. It was satisfying to see the Stars and Stripes fluttering over the trading post. We walked to the cafe, had a tremendous meal that included bananas for dessert. It had been more than a year since we had tasted a banana. Afterward, standing outside on the boardwalk, I caught our reflection in the cafe window and was shocked to see what we had become. Clothes worn—torn and filthy from a combination of animal blood, our own blood, campfire smoke, and ordinary dirt—and our faces black, we looked the part: authentic bush men. At a bar we had a couple drinks and went to bed, sleeping on the dock.

Early in the morning I was awakened by the robust whistle of the *S.S. Yukon*. I lay there watching as the ferry glided toward the dock like a duck, wings set, coming in to land at a pothole. Black smoke rolled from her smokestack, smudging the air. Tourists disembarked, women in long dresses, men in suits and vests, both sexes wearing mosquito netting over their heads. And the Indians lined up along the boardwalk, sitting cross-legged on blankets, playing Indian, selling the white tourists a remembrance of Fort Yukon: leather goods, fringed jackets, buckskin gloves, mukluks, and moccasins. Last night they had spoken English, but for the benefit of the tourists they spoke in their native dialect, aware it paid better to be a savage.

After a half-hour stop, the ferry continued upriver. Jeff and I watched the Indians count their money; then we bought needed

153

supplies and headed downstream. For three days, nearly 200 miles, we never saw another living soul until we came to a cabin sitting on a little bench above the river.

The cabin was crudely formed of driftwood pieced together and a roof of overlapping caribou hides. The door was a grizzly bear hide. It was readily apparent someone lived there; a fishing net was stretched over a bush, an ax was stuck in a chopping block. We yahooed without raising anyone.

We were curious and wanted to see the inside of the cabin. We pulled back the bear hide and stepped inside. Sunlight seeped between cracks in the wall, turning dust in the air to sparkles, but overall the interior was dark and mystifying. My eyes began adjusting. There was an old mattress on a pile of dry spruce boughs, a foot locker, and then I saw them—books—leather bound law books from the state of Illinois. There must have been at least a hundred volumes. They lined the walls on crudely-made shelves of driftwood and rocks. It was the ultimate shock to find such a fabulous law library in the wilds of Alaska.

The hair on the nape of my neck jumped. So peculiar, bizarre, curious. The owner was out there. I could feel him, sense him coming our way, coming slowly down a long gap in the pines, following the small creek that fed the swamp that leaked black water to the Pacific a gallon at a time. He startled several grouse that exploded from the lower branches of a spruce, and in a whirr of wings they circled the cabin and landed below near the river.

A magpie flew behind the cabin to challenge a pair of crows busy stripping meat off a fresh moose hide draped over a log. The crows chastised the intruder. And then there was the voice, the scream of a barbarous animal. "Bone pickers! Be gone!" It made my flesh crawl, and my saliva turned a bitter metallic taste.

He threw back the bear hide and came scrambling through the low doorway almost on all fours, a hairy, hulking figure carrying a rifle, returning to his lair. If he were able to stand straight, I was sure he would go seven foot. He was probably in his late 50s. His head was carried low on a thin neck. Obviously he was possessed. Black bushy beard. Eyes flashing. Licking lips. Red tongue. "Well, well." Wringing hands. "What do we have here?"

I spoke up, "We're the New York to Nome canoeists."

"The mad woodcutter," he told me, and his strange blue eyes glinted and narrowed. He wore a moose hide around his shoulders like a poncho, buckskin britches, and moccasins. "Hear that?" he wanted to know. All I could hear was the distant lament of wind in the trees. I shook my head.

"What?" Jeff wanted to know.

"Whoowhooowhooo," the woodcutter howled, and it made my

hackles jump. I thought to myself, "This fellow's nuts!"

He shook his head side to side, eyes showing white. He picked up a stick and rhythmically banged a center post which held up the roof. He chanted, "Social democrats. Social democrats. Everywhere . . . . Social democrats. Social democrats . . . ." He turned to me and wanted to know, "Are you . . ." His eyes blazed, and his voice was guttural, ". . . social democrats?"

"Hell, no," I informed him hastily. He smelled as rancid as fish heads left in the sun. Wanting to buy time, I asked, "How did you come by the law books?"

"Books?" he questioned. He was goofy. It didn't take a psychiatrist to tell.

"Whoowhooowhooo," he called, rolling his eyes. I now had it in my mind to attempt an escape, to ease around him. He leaned toward me, madness blinking neon-like. "They're trying to kill me. But they haven't yet. Trying to kill me," he raved.

I told the unfriendly giant, "Hey, it has been absolutely great having the opportunity to visit you. Thank you for extending us . . ." While I was talking, I motioned Jeff to go the other way around him. One of us might make it. ". . . your sincere hospitality. We have certainly appreciated it. But we are on an expedition of eminent importance and have to be going. We would love to stay . . . ."

"Don't go," he muttered, making a grab at my arm. I sidestepped and slithered around him. "There's social democrats out there. Stay away from social democrats."

Jeff and I scrambled topside and made tracks toward the canoe. I was trying to keep from running, hollering back to the mad woodcutter, "Your hospitality is unbelievable. We had a wonderful time. If everyone we met was like you, what a fantastic time we would have. Sorry we have to run, it's a long way to Nome. Thank you . . . ." When we reached *Muriel* I shut up. I had been talking more for myself, to keep calm, than anything else. That crazy bastard was behind us with a rifle. If we acted scared, he would blast us. I knew that instinctively. But if we went slow, if we acted a little crazy ourselves, if we put on a good show and departed quickly, he might not kill us.

I took my seat in *Muriel*. Jeff shoved off. I stole a quick peek, could see the black outline of the woodcutter with the rifle he held cradled in his arms, standing, skylined. If he wanted us we were dead meat. We headed down river with me in the stern, in the most vulnerable position. I would be first.

I whispered ahead to Jeff. "If that bastard pulls the trigger, you're on your own."

"Don't talk," he scolded.

I could feel sights lined on the small of my back and got a funny tickling sensation where shoulders blades met. If he squeezed off I would never know it. What would it feel like? Scorching metal slamming into me, velocity going from hundreds of feet per second to zero. Me taking the brunt of stopping it. Would it wallop when it hit? Would I scream? Would there be any pain? I shivered involuntarily. The hair on my neck stood on end. My lip twitched. Every ounce of strength I possessed was transmitted to the paddle in an effort to drive *Muriel* around the bend and out of harm's way.

CHAPTER 26

Two weeks running we averaged better than sixty miles a day, sailing and paddling down the Yukon. The few times we swung ashore, the mosquitoes made life so miserable we were soon back traveling. The weather held hot and humid. The sun, reflecting off the water, burned our eyes until color could no longer be distinguished. The world was black, white, gray.

From time to time we passed cabins and shacks; but not wanting to chance meeting another demented soul, we continued, stopping and resupplying at Eskimo settlements: Tanana, Galena, Anvik, Paimiut, Ohogamut, Andreafsky. Along the way the river emerged from the mountains and flattened out on a broad tundra flat. There were unattended fish wheels turning in the current, lifting salmon and dumping them into holding pens. There were eagles, owls, red-tailed hawks, foxes, and reindeer. Our diet consisted of whatever we chose to kill; it might be a reindeer or a snowshoe rabbit or a king salmon lifted from one of the traps. This was acceptable procedure for those traveling the Yukon.

We were swept downriver by a combination of current and wind. Gulls, cormorants, pelicans, grebs, and other coastal birds were numerous. I could sense salt water not far away. Behind us was 6,700 miles of travel in the wilds and now it was being expunged from our systems. I felt a close affinity for the interior, a raw, beautiful land, the people and their way of life.

We arrived at the settlement of Mountain Village, less than a hundred miles from the mouth of the Yukon, and were surprised by a delegation of people led by the school teachers, Mr. and Mrs. Sams. They had read about us in the newspapers, knew we would have to come through Mountain Village, and had been planning a celebration for over a year.

The celebration turned into a full-fledged party, with plenty of cold beer and even two beautiful nurses. At this stage of the journey I cannot imagine two young nurses who would not be beautiful. They smelled of jasmine, probably purchased from a catalog and delivered by mail. While we visited and drank, Mr. and Mrs. Sams prepared as close to a gourmet dinner as was possible in the Yukon.

At 3 A.M., with the midnight sun still shining brightly, I thanked Mr. and Mrs. Sams, told the nurses how much I enjoyed the evening, and prepared to leave. Drunk or sober, something in me tells me when it's time to leave, the proper moment. My motto is to leave people laughing, feeling good and wishing you could have stayed a little longer, rather than waiting until the party slackens and the booze begins to wear off. I suppose my sense of timing was gained from my being around the theater crowd in New York.

We no sooner got on the water and out of earshot than Jeff piped up with, "I don't see why we couldn't have stayed. We're almost to the ocean. We made it. Can't we slow down now?"

"You square-headed son of a bitch," I told him. It was alcohol doing most of the talking. "We've got Norton Sound to get around."

"Go to hell, Shell." What Jeff said next caught me off guard. "Ever since New York you've wanted to take a poke at me. So let's go ashore and settle this damn thing."

Man needs occasionally to fight with his fists for the same kind of natural reasons a wolf howls at the moon or a grouse dances before mating. We ran *Muriel* on shore and stripped off our mackinaws (the early morning had been cool), and tossed them over a windfall. Then Jeff and I squared off. Jeff assumed a classic defensive stance, crouched with his forearms and hands in position to block any assault. Jeff might have had me by a few inches and thirty pounds, but a Montana Red he was not. I took the offensive, threw a slapping jab, followed by a crisper jab that knocked his hand to the side. I saw an opening, cocked my right, and was about to unload it, when Jeff came with a sneak punch, a short left that caught me square on the point of my jaw. My legs buckled and, more from surprise than pain, I went down, plopped on my butt in the sand, undignified as hell. I sat there, lightning playing behind my eyes, bursts of yellow and streaks of orange colliding. I was looking up at the sky at Jeff's outline. He was pushing up his sleeves. He wanted more.

I spat blood, pushed myself off the ground, and told Jeff, "Lucky punch." He was crazy as a rabid dog if he thought otherwise. I circled, feinted twice, lunged, and tagged him with a right hook that smacked like a ripe watermelon dropped on pavement. Jeff went on his ass, the same as I had a few seconds earlier.

"We're even," I told him. "Get up."

We fought according to Marquis of Queensberry rules, civilized fighting, never trying to kill each other, only wanting to show who was the best man. I wanted to hurt him. I fought for pride, ego, self-esteem.

I knew I was a better boxer than Jeff, but didn't seem able to prove it. I had no power behind my punches, my timing was off. We fought to exhaustion and took a blow, sitting side by side leaned up against the windfall, sucking air, trying to work through the pain. I was tasting my blood. My head hurt. One eye was nearly swollen shut. Arms felt like leaden weights. Knuckles ached so that I wasn't sure I wanted to throw another punch.

I was hoping Jeff would call it quits but he did not, and we prepared to fight another round. We circled each other. I was embarrassed, embarrassed the fight had gone on so long, embarrassed I could not end it, embarrassed we were fighting at all. I stepped back, dropped my guard and told Jeff, "This is stupid. You sure as hell can't knock me out, and apparently I can't knock you out. It's a draw. Let's go."

We paddled *Muriel,* and for a long time I visualized the sounds of our slugging and our grunts and groans reverberating across the barren land and flashing across the slack water.

We were beginning to be influenced by ocean tides. Gulls wheeled and screamed overhead, geese on sandbars chatted and gossiped about us as we slid past. Frogs gave forth a polyphony of background sound, and a bald eagle hung on the silent wind. The wind, cool, fresh out of the west, carried the tang of salt water and kelp and the traces of sea life: migrating whales, sea lions, clams blowing bubbles in the sand.

Never had it entered my thick skull that Jeff could stand up to me in a fist fight. I sobered a little, and that only made the scene in my memory all the more painful.

Jeff broke the silence between us. "Let's make camp."

"We'll make camp when I decide to," I groused, saying it to make the point that we had had a scrap but nothing was changed. If there was a serious decision to be made, I would make it just as I always had. No coin flip. No bullshit. We went another three miles before I steered toward a gravel beach. Too exhausted and beat up to fiddle with the tent, we lay on the ground and pulled the tent over us.

I awoke a few hours later feeling lousy, lousy, lousy. The sun was shining through the canvas giving a green underwater effect. I looked over and there, only a few scant inches from me, was Jeff. His face looked as though it had been run through a sausage grinder. His eyes were open. I must have looked equally bad. I don't know which of us started laughing first—I think we tied. It was one of the few times we laughed together. It felt good, but it hurt.

"How dumb," I told him.

"Sure was."

"But it was kind of fun, too, wasn't it? Maybe it was good we were drunk. Otherwise we might have really gotten hurt."

CHAPTER 27

The fight brought obvious damage: physical pain and emotional strain. In my heart I knew I had failed and failed miserably. But by far the most discomforting outgrowth of the fight was that we had walked away and left our mackinaws draped over the windfall. We did not realize it until the next day, and with a strong easterly wind blowing, it would have cost us a day to go back. Anyway, I didn't want to go back and witness the marks in the sand telling a most pathetic chapter in the saga of the New York to Nome expedition.

As we drew closer to the ocean, shivering in the rain, there were several times *Muriel* was rocked as if we had run up and over something; then a spray of water would follow and a horrible stench. This happened several times before we came alongside a fisherman in a power boat who informed us beluga whales, traveling in pods of eight or ten, were chasing salmon upstream. He laughed and said a male had probably nudged our canoe with romance on his mind.

Before reaching Norton Sound, the Yukon River fragmented; we took the first channel on our starboard and made a run toward Pastol Bay. The country around us was flat tundra, very green and dotted by outbursts of colorful wildflowers. To the east, far in the distance, was a thin line of blue mountains, a misty veil stretched over them. There was not a tree, not so much as a bush in sight. Grebes dove underwater as we approached, and long lines of tundra swans passed overhead, their voices a melodic woo-wooing. Herring gulls circled overhead going gah-gah-gah. There were long Vs of Canadian honkers, and the ducks I was able to identify included mallards, canvasbacks, pintails, buffleheads, scoters, and mergansers. The mouth of the Yukon was a feathered sanctuary.

The Pastol Bay Eskimos came to the beach, crowded around

161

to stare at *Muriel*. They shook their heads and said over and over, "No good." They showed us their own crafts, umiaks, and said an open craft like *Muriel* would not stand a chance in the ocean. I was dreading the ocean travel because I did not know what to expect, and the Eskimos' comments did little to instill me with confidence.

Our charts indicated shoals and hinted at channels. We found the shoals but not the channels. The tide was out and the water too shallow to paddle. We waded mile after mile across a mudflat, pulling *Muriel*, occasionally dropping into holes that would dunk us.

Gradually the water lost the muddy brown to which we were accustomed and turned to an inkiness. Kelp floated on the surface, and we felt a vague sensation of swells, of water building under us and letting down as if it were a chest rising and falling with regular breathing. We were able to paddle again, and we kept busy holding *Muriel* in the push of the wind and the pull of the tide.

A strange thing occurred after we reached the sea. We were bone-weary, our bruised bodies hurting, and the sun about to drop from the sky for a few minutes of dusk. Small scattered islands were silhouetted against the orange and yellow water, and all around us salmon leaped with tireless enthusiasm, as if electrified. I could not understand this strange phenomenon until just about the time the sun was ready to reappear, when a number of curious seals popped to the surface and traveled along with us for a distance.

When we finally set camp, it was in a ceaseless downpour. We put up the tent and crawled into eiderdown bags that were reduced to the thickness and warmth of wet sheets. We passed a few dismal hours that way, and then I rolled out and managed to get a fire going.

Not once did I offer myself congratulations for reaching the Pacific. To me, the drive to reach Nome, the striving toward our singular goal, was all-consuming. I wanted to get there, period.

We reached the Eskimo village of St. Michael where the skeletal remains of several dozen derelicts littered the bay at low tide. On shore were shacks pieced together with wood and tin. The natives met us, showed us their kayaks and umiaks, and again we were informed an open boat such as *Muriel* would surely be sunk in the water we were to face. We purchased what we needed at the trading post, paying horribly inflated prices, and went on our way.

From St. Michael the shoreline became rugged, and there was a sheer rock wall, sometimes a thousand feet high, that seemed to extend to infinity. We stood out a quarter mile or so from shore, so we would not be battling the backwash, and sailed against deep ground swells and a lively chop. We managed to keep a taut sail and a bending mast. To the west, water and sky appeared welded, and to the east, the rugged cliff sealed us from the continent. There were no friendly beaches, only waves crashing against the cliff. If a bad storm caught us, if there were a sudden squall, we would be left to survive on our skill as canoeists—and luck. How we had changed from the two novices who sank the first day on the Hudson!

Later the wind died and we took up the paddles. The world slowed to the regular beat of the waves building, building, exhaling. Sea birds emerged from the rocky cliff as we passed, swooping over us for a better view, flying out to sea before circling behind. Northern fulmars were identified by the barrel roll effect they made skimming the water and then rising high in the air before dropping again to the surface to repeat the procedure. Puffin, so numerous it sometimes appeared the cliffs were falling on us, would drop and fly off, their stocky black bodies pushing their brilliant orange bills in front of them. Terns, graceful and gull like, dove for fish. Rafts of murres parted. Guillemots swooped low, singing their cry, peeee-peeeee-peeeee. And from time to time the belugas would find us, spout and perform 360 degree rolls, I suppose to try and entice us to join their fun.

When we absolutely had to locate breaks in the seawall, to fix a bite to eat or because the wind was kicking up, it seemed we were always able to find where a river had cut through the rock. At the base there would be a spit where we could get away from the ocean. It seemed the divine hand of guidance was with us.

After we passed the mouth of Cascade Creek, the rock wall began to taper toward tundra country. Twelve miles from the settlement of Unalakleet, we got out on the beach to shoot some movie footage of a huge bull walrus. Inadvertently I happened to leave the Kodak camera on a rock, and it was only after reaching Unalakleet that I realized it. We lost travel time because we had to hire a fellow with a boat and a kicker to run me back. While he waited, Jeff met Mr. and Mrs. Swenson, school teachers who took us in. They fed us, and we took a bath and went to bed. It was the first time we had slept in a bed with sheets since the Albert Hotel in Winnipeg the year before. It was heavenly to lie there between the cool, ironed sheets and feel the tactile sensations over my freshly scrubbed body. I had even shaved and given myself a haircut.

Of course, in the morning we had to have breakfast and visit with the Swensons, and we therefore got a late start. Before we departed, Mr. Swenson said he would radio to the settlements ahead and to Nome that we were headed their way.

At Cape Darby we were forced two miles off shore because of low tide and a mudflat. As we rounded the point, a southeaster caught us, shook us, and drove us toward the beach where we were able to make camp in the lee of a small alder thicket. A rain shower passed over and we stayed hunkered in our tent. After it passed, since the seas were too high to navigate, we went on a hunting expedition. I carried the gun. We had gone from camp only a quarter mile or so when we surprised two small reindeer. I shot one in the head and he dropped, but he got up and had to be bulldogged.

I was on the ground struggling with the reindeer. He had one hind foot in my front pocket and was about to make me a gelding. I hollered at Jeff, "Cut his throat!" He tried to use his knife like a saw and I snapped at him, "Stick the goddamn point in." He finally did and succeeded in killing the animal. We dressed the little deer and laid the meat on the tundra grass to cool. We sat having a smoke. We were both quiet. I was feeling the first twinges of thoughtfulness—if the weather held a few more days we would be in Nome. Perhaps I was supposed to feel happy we were so close but actually I was regretting that this wonderful way of life was about to end.

The next settlement was Golifin. We were met on the beach by the entire white population, including Mr. and Mrs. Folger, the Reverend Kimbal and his wife, and two brothers, Joe and Jimmie Dexter, after whom Point Dexter was named. We spent the night with the Dexter brothers who had come to Alaska during the gold rush in '98. Now Joe was ninety-two and Jimmie eighty-one. We sat in their cabin drinking bourbon, listening to stories about locating placer pockets and the pleasure of spending sprees.

The following morning, Sunday, a special breakfast was held for Jeff and me. Mrs. Kimbal arranged it, and everyone, white and Eskimo alike, attended. At the head table the centerpiece was a paper canoe filled with flowers and a banner proclaiming "New York to Golifin." After that, we were obliged to stay while Reverend Kimbal led Sunday service.

As a result, it was noon before we were able to tear ourselves away. That day we made a measly twenty-two miles. The next day we added twenty-five miles, and the last full day of the expedition we managed thirty miles, setting camp a scant ten miles shy of Nome.

In the morning the sun shone as brightly as it ever had during the past sixteen months. The blue in the sky stretched to infinity.

The water was flat as glass except for the dimpling effect of the roll and pitch of the waves and their gentle slapping on shore.

We got underway and decided rather than sneaking along shore like a couple of cheechakos, we would swing out and come in the channel.

And so we did. We swung a mile out and started the bottom half of the arc to our destination. This then was the final leg. The expedition was ending. Jeff was a dark shadow, and the shoreline a blur of brown beach and green tundra flats. And streaming from the buildings toward the shore where we would land was what looked to be the entire population of Nome. In my mind's eye I recalled Mackenzie, the ice of Great Slave Lake, buffalo hunting, the moody water of Superior. How many portages had we been over? I remembered the mosquitoes and deerflies and no-see-ums. Remembered all the times we had surprised a bull moose or a bear, getting so close it would sometimes scare the hell out of us. Remembered the crazy, wonderful call of the loon, the lonely howl of a wolf on a moonlit night with the northern lights playing. Remembered the mist lying like gossamer over the water and the ducks out there talking back and forth. It had been so damned perfect. But it was ending. The challenge had been met.

EPILOGUE

August 11, 1987. It does not seem possible that it has been fifty years to the day since Jeff and I completed our expedition of discovery. Until now it has been an untold story, primarily because in our absence the world continued to spin. In 1936 and 1937 the economy was improving, and people were returning to work. So much happened while we were out of touch. The German dirigible *Hindenburg* exploded in New Jersey. The Golden Gate bridge, the longest suspension bridge in the world, was opened. Aviator Amelia Earhart vanished on an around-the-world flight. Joe Lewis became the world heavyweight champion. But more than anything else, it was Adolph Hitler, rearming Germany and laying claim to neighboring territory, that made the public turn away from following the adventures of a couple of canoeists. They were more worried about hanging on to their jobs and surviving the world war that seemed inevitable.

From Nome we took the *S.S. Victoria* to Seattle, and from there we flew to New York. We never bothered with Wiegers but did manage to sign a contract for a movie and a book with the William Morris agency. But those projects dragged on for several months. Jeff moved back to Minneapolis, and finally I just said to hell with it and hopped a freighter heading for Hawaii.

The only thing I really regret is that *Muriel* was never given the distinction she deserved, a display at the Smithsonian. She was shipped from Seattle to New York. I never claimed her. She went for demurrage.

In Hawaii I visited my folks. And I met and married the most beautiful girl on the islands, Dora. I started the Home Beverage Company and landed the retail franchise for Coca Cola on the island of Oahu. It was a company with a great future but then came December 7, 1941—Pearl Harbor—and the Army took over my trucks.

After the war I went to work for the Honolulu Paper Company and spent the next twenty years working in the paper industry in Hawaii and on the West Coast, as my father, grandfather, great-grandfather and great-great-grandfather had done.

In 1967 I retired, and Dora and I moved into a home with acreage in the Sierra Nevada mountains about seventy miles northwest of Reno. I like the country around here. At times it vaguely reminds me of the Canadian bush.

Since I retired, we have traveled extensively. One summer we visited Fort Smith. There were even a few people I remembered, though not many. The country had changed, and that was the biggest disappointment to me. Back in the mid-'30s, when Jeff and I came through, the only means of transportation was the canoe, the same as it had been in Mackenzie's day. There were a few float planes, but mainly it was the canoe. Now there are roads everywhere. There are roads to McMurray, Chipewyan, Smith, Resolution. Even a road to Aklavik above the Arctic Circle. I try to explain what it was like, but it is impossible because it was a feeling more than anything else. They have taken the wild out of it.

Jeff and I have kept in touch off and on over the years. He went back to Minneapolis and had a career selling women's and baby clothing. Every few years one of us will call the other. At first the conversation will be strained. After a while we get to reminiscing about the expedition. I always feel a little melancholy after talking to Jeff.

He was one type of guy, one personality, and I was another. I've given it considerable thought over the years and have decided we were the perfect blend to make the expedition a success. If we had both been like him, we would still be paddling up the Hudson. And if we were both like me, we probably would have driven each other into the ground. The blend, the team, it worked.

Two things I will always be grateful for—being born and living during such an eventful and historical time, and making it to Nome.

POSTSCRIPT

The 1974 *Guinness Book of World Records* listed our expedition as the "longest canoe trip in history." It listed the date of departure, April 25, 1936, from New York City and our arrival at Nome on August 11, 1937.

Several years later our record was replaced by kayakers. That is strictly bull. Kayaks should be a separate class. The way I look at it, in addition to being the discoverers of a waterway across North America, we still hold the record for the longest canoe trip in history. I wear a gold ring that says "World Record." That is how proud I am of it.

ABOUT THE AUTHOR

RICK STEBER, The Northwest's favorite storyteller, is a native of the high desert country of eastern Oregon. A graduate of Southern Oregon State College, Steber worked toward a master's degree in public administration at the University of Oregon before joining the staff of Mayor Terry Schrunk of Portland. Later he worked as a labor relations consultant for city and county governments.

"When I was young, growing up in Bonanza, the old-timers told me stories about ranching, logging, and Indian wars. When they died, they took those stories to their graves. This seemed inherently wrong," said Steber. "More than any other reason, with the idea that with the passing of these people we were losing the backbone of our history, it prompted me to dedicate myself to becoming a writer."

In 1973 Steber began writing a syndicated newspaper column called "Oregon Country," a series of historical vignettes from the Northwest. He searched out and interviewed pioneers, stage drivers, lawmen, teachers, and other old-timers. Their stories were published in "Oregon Country," magazine articles, and Steber's books *Rendezvous*, *Traces*, *Wild Horse Rider*, *Union Centennial*, *Where Rolls the Oregon*, and the Old Oregon Country Series, a collection of stories from his column.

In his newest book, *New York to Nome, The Northwest Passage by Canoe*, Steber tells the story of two young men who battle the elements and themselves to complete an epic canoe journey across the continent. Steber met Shell Taylor, from whose recollections the story is told, after an appearance on a California television program discussing one of his books. Taylor felt a "kindred spirit" with Steber and immediately called the television studio proposing the two meet to discuss "a canoe trip of high adventure." The resulting interviews and research for the book took ten years.

Steber's writing shows an empathy for his characters and a love for the land in which they live. His detailed descriptions liven the senses and increase understanding of the human spirit. His research often leads him to share the experiences of the characters he writes about, whether hiking the Oregon Trail, canoeing through the wilderness, or riding horseback.

Reluctant to label himself strictly as a historian, Steber says, "You could probably call what I do a combination of historian, biographer, and storyteller. Most of all, I like to tell a good story, to give a reader a sense of what it was like to be there."

Rick Steber lives near Prineville, Oregon, with his wife, Kristi, and sons, Luke and Dusty. He works at a studio-cabin in the Ochoco Mountains.